THE YEAR

THE YEAR

by

LORD DUNSANY

JUNE

June 14

June, and the time has come for cutting hay.
    Far off with its tremendous pageantry
The agony and splendour of this day
    Flare over Europe. But in Ireland see
    Only the deep grass waving, and a tree
Sheltering jackdaws, from which they descend
    To search the swathes that man's machinery,
Aided by horses, lays at the field's end,
And tall beyond it still the hay's brown heads extend.

1944

2

Brown is the field, but as the wind goes by
    A wave of silver seems to travel it.
Green lie the swathes. In pairs the swallows fly
    Low over them to catch whatever flit
    From their small fallen houses. Bit by bit
The tall grass narrows, though a corncrake still
    Calls from what was her home since she alit
First from her world-wide journey ; all the ill
Invaded peoples fear touches her with its thrill.

3

Man has his uses. This I can record
    From having watched a jackdaw, whose grey head
Bends now so eagerly above the hoard
    That men have just laid bare ; with keen swift tread
    He searches in the treasure that is shed
Upon the ground, or in the earth laid bare.
    And now, from neighbouring trees and towers sped,
His comrades have come sailing down to share
The wealth which Man has cast in such profusion there.

4

A pheasant on her nest with all her eggs
    Are in the deadly way of the machine,
Which passes over, cutting off her legs.
    This is a curse that is well shared between
    Man and all other creatures : we have been
Slaughtered as much by what we thought our slave
    (Who does not serve us as we had foreseen)
As the poor creatures whom the long grass gave
A shelter, till there came what never cares to save.

5

I can remember hayfields to which men
    Came with their scythes long since, when large and white
The dog-daisies were grown ; in valleys then
    Far from the towns they dwelt, and saw the light
    Of noon and gloaming soft and wide ; or bright
The clear stars shone for them, and windows glowed
    Only to beautify the Summer night,
And not to drive it thence ; the large moths showed
To them their golden eyes, sailing their own wild road.

6   *June* 15

Each June they saw the roses come again
    In wild wood gardens, or at a field's end
Saw their fair faces peer along a lane,
    And the great foxglove was to them a friend.
    They knew the time when hazel boughs would bend
With ripened nuts. They knew the time of year
    Not from a printed date, but from the trend
Of Nature's self ; wild voices in their ear
Told more of the year's march then ever towns may hear.

7

Then the machine came : one man reaped a field
    Where ten had worked. No more the meadowlands
Had work for nine of them : the harvest's yield
    Was gathered up and stacked by iron hands.
    There came Prosperity, with its demands
For labour, but to serve the grim machine.
    From vale and upland went unhappy bands
To work where sun and moon are seldom seen
And where the flowers and birds they knew, had never been.

Over high houses in the afternoon
    The sun set early ; memories of wings
And leaves, and nightingales beneath the moon,
      And owls and moths, seemed like fantastic things,
      And only pavement real : clatterings
Rose from machines, the voices of the hills
    Seemed faint and far ; only imaginings
Of poets spoke to them of fields and rills.
Far, far from them were woods that knew the blackbirds' trills.

             9

I know not what a moth or star can teach,
    Or what a man may learn from a wild rose,
The blackbirds' chorus or the white owl's screech ;
      But this, whate'er it be, was learned by those
      No longer ; as a man by German foes
Taken to work, they worked for what had won
    Where they had lost, and learned the alien prose
Of the machine, the bitter lore that none
Shall ever profit by till cogs and shafts are done.

            10   *June* 16

That was long since. And now not all is lost.
    Towns have not covered all the countryside,
Or summoned all men to them. Still is tossed
      Like a victorious banner floating wide
      The white-thorn every May, and still abide
The splendours of the seasons, whose scouts creep
    Up to the edge of cities, which deride
These ancient things in the brief time they keep
Their hold, to follow soon great Babylon to sleep.

            11

Still we mow fields, if not with the old lore.
    And now the meadow that I watch is mown,
And green lie thirty swathes, brown thirty more,
      As t'wards us or away they have been thrown.
      The corncrake from her home is lately flown
To safer shelter, where her brood finds cover,
    Small black round things that for few days have grown.
Fallen are buttercups, their summer over,
Dog-daisies, tottie grass, and white and crimson clover.

A lazy stream runs near, where herons fish,
 And yellow wagtails run along the mud,
Catching as many insects as they wish.
  Above the water, shadowed by a wood,
  Small flies are dancing, lighted by a flood
Of sunlight through the darkness of the trees,
  As planets in the night. Now is in bud
Portuguese laurel : elder scents the breeze
And the tall monkshood blooms ; and now awake the bees.

In garden borders blooms the Austrian rose,
 And cottage gardens gleam with clematis,
And honeysuckle over doorways glows ;
  Now all along the roads the wild rose is,
  A deeper pink where once stood cottages,
Remembering gardens that have passed away,
  Child of some richer rose ; small companies
Of orchids to the roadside now display
Their beauty, and a few are fallen with the hay.

14

The yellow iris shines by streams, and all
 Through marshy places ; like an elfin king
With purple robe the foxglove rises tall
  Over the other flowers. Blossoming
  Is the syringa, and the evening
Is odorous with scent. Summer is here
  When the syringa blooms. Wing upon wing,
Swallows sail high. Sweetwilliams now appear.
When their bright flowers are seen, the longest day is near.

15

The hay is turned, but not by human hands.
 We cannot work with speed of the machine.
Man was the chiefest, once, of all earth's bands.
  A greater power now is on the scene.
  And, like the monsters of the Pleiocene,
We've had our turn ; our own grim progeny
  Is the world's master now, as Man had been.
Perhaps our final conquerors will be
Pilotless planes, to sweep our towns from memory.

16

And yet, as wander to a battlefield,
    When armies have retired from it or died,
Wild creatures creeping in from wold and weald,
    To live there where the hush lies deep and wide,
    Forgetting one fierce day ; man simplified
May be the heir of too precocious man
    And on the wreck of our old rails abide
And dust of cities, caring not to scan
The intricacies or the wonder of our plan.

17   *June* 19

The hay is partly gathered up next day
    In Irish haycocks nearly eight feet high,
Of which the jackdaws have a lot to say
    All through the evening, though I know not why ;
    And men with pitchforks, their day not gone by
Quite utterly, shared work with the machine,
    As, near the ending of their history,
In this same meadow there may once have been
A few last Irish elks still lingering on the scene.

18   *June* 20

The shining beauty of the Spring has faded
    Out of the beech-leaves, but blue shadows dream
In hollows of far woods. Where ways are shaded
    By woods that hang above the herons' stream
    An avalanche of sunlight is agleam
On slopes of branches, and among them rise
    . Dark evergreens that like green shadows seem.
There like a broken chip from Paradise
A kingfisher upon his daily journey flies.

19   *June* 21

As daylight dimmed I saw a brown owl roaming
    Over the field from which the hay is gone ;
And silently into the silent gloaming
    With slow beats of his wings he floated on.
    All day upon the fields the sun had shone,
And now the haycocks all stand neatly tied
    With ropes of straw. Mauve and vermilion
Now fuchsias droop by walks, and now beside
A hayfield rises up a mullein in its pride.

And pigeons from a farmyard share the treasure
    Stored in the ground the long knife has laid bare,
With rooks and jackdaws, wealth we cannot measure
    Or even notice, and there seek it there
    Creatures of whom our eyes are unaware,
Small things whose presence we can only trace
    From the brown kestrel's slant along the air
Down to the hayfield. Now the sun's long race
Northward is done, and South he turns his fiery face.

21

For fifty yards acacia scents the air,
    Now that its bloom is gleaming. A high wall
Runs round a garden where bright lupins flare
    By marigolds and pansies and the small
Bloom of veronica. Irises stand tall.
Thousands of strawberries redden and expand
    And the anemone's last petals fall
And trees lean over, peering at the land
So different from the wild rough soil on which they stand.

22

And by their feet the ragged-robins team
    Wild and unkempt, so near to the proud roses
Beyond the wall, and spotted orchids gleam
    Pale in the grass, flowers no man encloses
    In garden walls, though some he thus disposes
Are scarcely fairer than these orchids are,
    These children of the wild. And now reposes
On trellis made of wooden post and bar
White clematis that shines in green shade like a star.

23

Two rows of Irish yews guard the decay
    Of an old garden, and beyond them rise
Green fountains that from forests far away
    Were brought to Irish soil. Stone steps surprise
    A wanderer through the grass, and then his eyes
Fall on white statues, which seem not to know
    How long the weeds have reigned, or that time flies
Over the flower-beds of long ago,
Time that brings weeds and moss, and loves to see them grow.

I picture Liberty, the gods' fair daughter,
    Marching with mighty strides through the Atlantic,
East from America, knee-deep in water,
    And rising from it on the old, romantic,
    Orchard-clad, Norman coast, and with gigantic
Thunder of blows on Cherbourg striking down
    An army of a tyrant, while his frantic
Boasts, threats and lies grow fainter, till they drown
In meaningless complaints beneath a thwarted frown.

25

June 23

For news has come to-day of the impending
    Fall of that fortress on the Norman coast
Which a doomed German corps is still defending
    Against the men of Eisenhower's host,
    Whose fame sounds even here, though Meath almost
Sleeps through this summer, deaf to the world's cries
    Struggling for liberty against the boast
Of Hitler, heedless of its agonies
And not exalted by the light in free men's eyes.

26

This is St. John's eve, and a holy well
    Draws many who will visit it to-night
At midnight, sacred, as the legends tell,
    From times before St. John ; and there by light
    Of stars when a young moon is sunk from sight
They will seek cures for troubles that alarm
    The flesh and blood, and help against what fight
To overthrow the soul ; and find a charm
In Warrenstown, we hope, to guard them against harm.

27

After the news of these historic days
    We listen to Beethoven. What were all
The seven wonders of the old world's praise
    Compared to wireless ? What the ancient wall
    From which hung gardens ? What the tomb and pall
    Of Mausolus, or that to which they bore
    Cheops ? Jove's statue, or Diana's hall ?
Or the colossus guarding Rhodes of yore,
Or Ptolemy's bright light that guided ships to shore ?

Not how the ancients would have looked in awe
    Upon our wonder let us meditate,
But what this strange thing will have power to draw
    From our own days. Let our age estimate
    The hold it has on us. It gave a State
To a dictator, who had never been,
    Without Marconi's aid, so elevate
On such a height, as that where he is seen
To stand with giddy feet above the last ravine.

29

Kings, conquests, explorations, laws, of old
    Shaped not the fortunes of humanity
As our inventions have us in their hold,
    To shape the destinies of men to be.
    We scarcely understand the ones we see
Around us. Man is like a child at play
    Among strange weapons. What catastrophe
Will come of it we have no power to say,
And the strange weapons grow in number day by day.

30

Again I saw a kingfisher go by
    Above dull water, an unearthly blue.
No brighter colour between earth and sky
    Moves in these disunited isles. It flew
    Straight down the middle of the stream, and through
The gloom and gleam of trees. Its splendour went
    Like a bright dream illumining anew
A life grown grey in streets, or an event
Brilliant and unforeseen where all was somnolent.

31 *June 25*

Low fly the swallows, prophesying rain
    Or chasing flies the damp air presses low,
And the rain comes, which jackdaws count a gain,
    To judge from their loud voices where they go
    Over the hayfield. Near them a grey crow
Pecks at a piece of offal ; body pale
    All over, as a lump of street-soiled snow ;
Jet-black his head and wings and claws and tail.
To scavenge many lands his harsh-voiced comrades sail.

The golden water-lily in the Boyne
 Is shining now, and where a grove had been,
Of beech now cut, and Boyne and Claddy join,
 A company of mulleins may be seen
 Rising up tall, that had not known the sheen
Of so much sunlight when the beeches stood.
 Gone is the lovely leafage of that screen,
But some amends are made for the lost wood
By the pale yellow glow of this half-elfin brood.

33

With faces sometimes pink and sometimes pale
 Now the wild roses in the hedgerows teem.
Reedy and low the Boyne lies in his vale,
 The yellow iris brighter than his stream.
 Hiding among their leaves his waters seem,
Which soon will rise up higher than them all
 And answer to the cold sky, gleam for gleam,
Fed with the rains that in December fall
When snipe are by his banks and teal and wigeon call.

We, like an insect walking on a page
 Of some great book, see dimly history
Which to the children of a future age
 A logical and simple tale shall be,
 Effect succeeding cause consistently,
A jigsaw fitted in, which now is lying
 Scattered about us. Italy grows free.
Cherbourg is fallen. Hitler's troops are flying
In Russia, and men see that tyranny is dying.

35

And yet June, heedless of the rage of man,
 Heedless of ruin of his homes and hers,
Goes on from day to day with her old plan,
 Watching the seed-pods ripen on the furze,
 Seeing the sun at evening reverse
His northward journey, events great and small
 Seemingly one to her : where conifers
Lean their long arms over a garden wall
Snapdragons start to shine and poppy-petals fall.

36

Last night a gray mist risen from a stream
    Floated across the fields, when cocks of hay
Were like large seated gnomes, and still a gleam
    Lingered on earth from the departed day.
    And owls began to mutter, and a ray
Shone from a young moon faintly, and a sigh
    Of Autumn reached us though from far away,
A hint, a threat, a whispered prophecy,
That in a little while the Summer flowers would die.

37   *June 28*

Now in the garden raspberries turn red
    Upon the sunny side, and figs appear,
And now the columbine has drooped her head
    And petals of the guelder rose are sere,
    And the pale blue companula is here :
Cherries blush faintly, little pears are brown,
    And currants get some colour, as the year
Past midsummer begins the long slant down
To autumn's friendly smile and then December's frown.

38   *June 29*

The lovely amaryllis under glass
    Is gleaming still : love-in-a-mist arises :
The rhododendron's petals strew the grass :
    The lupin with his many bright surprises
    Of colour, like an elf in ten disguises,
Grows seed-pods now.   Clematis, standing tall
    Over the garden, wakes ; and one surmises
That soon a dark-blue cataract will fall,
Glowing like Summer skies, down the old garden-wall.

39

Along a pergola which roses climb
    Wisteria is still a mass of flowers,
And honeysuckle, but both past their prime,
    And in a little while over those bowers
    The rose alone will reign through shining hours,
Watching the sun go southward from these lands.
    A little company of foxgloves dowers
With beauty a low weedy mound that stands
Where an old rock-garden was made by unknown hands.

This is the end of June, a month that meant
    So much to Liberty, in exile still.
Last night a murmur through the midnight went,
    A faint memorial of sounds that fill
    The skies of Kent, where we heard battle thrill
The air and save the world.   But Ireland sleeps
    And knows not who went by above the hill
Roaming the midnight through the starry deeps,
But dully hears the news and neither cheers nor **weeps.**

B

JULY

1

Here comes July. And stately in the gloom
   Of aged laurels lifts the Turk's-cap lily
With all its dark-pink flowers now in bloom ;
     Five feet in height, and far too starched and frilly
     To roam so free. From some wild land and hilly
Its sires had come into captivity,
     And then escaped. Now where the birds sing shrilly
It is as wild, once more, as they can be,
Outside the garden's walls, lovely, alone and free.`

2

And through the laurels and across the grass
   A pea-hen walks demurely with her brood ;
Her neck in sunlight glitters like green brass.
     Now where the haycocks up to eight feet stood
     Their shapes are shrunk, as though a brotherhood
Of gnomes had all grown old : with greater store
     Of wisdom they look now to be endued,
With greater treasure of mysterious lore,
As evening's solemn hush creeps round them more and more.

3

Now blooms the borage in its garden-bed,
   Which wild on Kentish hill-slopes wanderers see,
Slopes over which blind bombs are being sped
     On missions of revenge for agony
     Now suffered by a fallen tyranny,
Fallen but living, like the smitten snake
     Which dies at sunset, as the peasantry
Of downlands used to say. Soon death will take
Him who fed Death so well, now that his armies break.

4

And, while those armies break by Russian streams,
  Listlessly grow the plants of which I tell.
Far outside history are these my themes ;
  The garden and the hay, the holy well,
  And meadowlands that never heard a shell.
And in those meadows grass and flowers grow,
  Where no sound louder than the chapel bell
Stirs the deep peace and liberty we owe
To those who guard these things, men that we do not know.

5

And in that idle and untroubled hush
  Now the sweet-peas display their shining faces,
And sometimes, creeping low, with rustic blush,
  Pink flowers flourish in deserted places,
  The sweet-peas' poor relations ; these are traces
Of gardens that have been, where homes have gone,
  And still these flowers live, remembering graces
Where once were paths along which roses shone,
With marigolds and pinks for them to look upon.

6

And now the larkspur rises tall and bright,
  Bluer than skies that over Delphi glow,
From which he takes a name more erudite
  Than that plain English name he used to know.
  The scented purple stock begins to show.
And now the regal rose, queen of the garden,
  Whose buds I should have praised some days ago,
Comes to her splendour, and I ask their pardon.
Unrivalled she will reign till frosts begin to harden.

7   *July 2*

And now a wet day comes. For long has swept
  Rain like a pale ghost with a pale grey tress,
As though the Irish guardian angels wept,
  Not for our sins, but out of weariness
  And utter boredom at our listlessness
In times when earth and heaven elsewhere ring,
  Heaven with a high cause, and earth with stress
Of battle (which some bard is yet to sing)
In lands whence Liberty has long been wandering.

And in the weary tears the angels weep
   The earth grows dreary and no poet sings.
No more makes Pegasus his upward leap
   Through clear bright air, but on earth droops his wings,
   Delaying among transitory things.
For rain may beat against a spirit's flight,
   As it may check an army's thunderings
And give historians a date to write
Days hence for some advance men planned to make to-night.

9

Yet let us not be dulled by a wet day.
   There is a concert-hall in Paris where
I hear a symphony, then cross the way
   Into Vienna for some Austrian air
   And stroll to Spain to hear Beethoven there
And, coming home by Tunis, hear the song
   That Arabs sing beside their tents of hair ;
For we can do these wonders who belong
To that strange century whose magic is so strong.

10

And there's the magic Caxton gave the world,
   Which he had got from Faust and Faust from Hell,
Into whose fires his soul had to be hurled,
   If all is true that the old legends tell.
   And some there are to-day who sense the smell
Of everlasting fire round printer's ink.
   But, be that as it may, if one choose well,
The rain may fall until the haycocks sink :
Choose ill, and one may lose in time the power to think.

11

I chose to-day that luminous Russian soul
   Gleaming among black shadows fiercely blown
By stormy passions to an aimless goal,
   Fyodor Dostoevsky, who has known
   The hearts of men as if they were his own,
Whom only Tolstoy rivalled in his day.
   What writers were those Russians ! Who have shown
Their countryside to us so far away
That we can almost see the woods and smell the hay.

The rain is gone and Canterbury bells
    Swing to make music that the flowers hear ;
A bud on a Madonna lily swells
    To flower overnight, and somewhere near
    Geraniums in their bright coats appear.
In a small garden, now no longer tended,
    Violas rise among the weeds to cheer
Some little rocks beside a fence unmended,
And daphne's berries there are shining red and splendid.

Browner appear the haycocks for the rain,
    And greener the grass round them : still they keep
That look of grave old gnomes. Wet bodes again,
    For low over the grass the swallows sweep,
    While the last shadows of the evening creep.
Now the tremendous news that Minsk is taken
    Comes through the ether, as the Russians reap
A victory that through the world will waken
High hopes in hearts of all but those by heart forsaken.

Now what the swallows prophesied is here,
    A misty shower narrowing the view,
As though an even thicker bandage were
    Tied over Ireland's eyes lest she see through
    And do what talkers would not have her do.
A company of white campanulas,
    Which in the night to their full stature grew,
Gleam in the dark of trees, as though there has
Appeared an elfin troop where weedy stillness was.

I saw to-day, drifted against a yew
    A shrub called snow-in-summer : what its name
In latin at full length I never knew,
    But some way off it seems the very same
    As any snow that in December came.
Like a night full of stars syringa glows
    And dahlias have just begun to flame.
Wild in a wood the deadly nightshade grows,
Hanging its sombre bells where heavy shades repose.

16

Now a convolvulus lifts up its head,
    Climbing an old wall, and near by is seen
Cotoneaster's berries turning red
    Among its little leaves of darkest green.
    Portuguese laurel's proudest hour has been,
And rhododendron's glory is all over,
    And heavily the boughs in orchards lean,
And clouds of flies begin to hum and hover,
Till through the dark sails home the heron, that old rover.

17

A chestnut sheltered by an ancient mound,
    Built for defence by men of days unknown,
Has leaned its heavy branches to the ground,
    Where they make chairs, upholstered as through strown
    With green silk by the moss upon them grown ;
And over it a kestrel sails, intent
    On fields below his blue and cloudy zone,
Where swallows soar towards the way he went,
As I have seen rooks do when bombs were over Kent.

18

Meadowsweet buds where rushes still remember
    An old lake long since dry, though sometimes yet,
When rain has soaked the meadows all December
    And January's days are gray and wet,
    The lake comes back where under suns long set
It used to shine.   And now, all round, the thistle
    Defies Man's tidiness that would forget
The ancient wild, and on his stalk of gristle
Lifts high above the grass his threatening thorny bristle.

19

In a sand-quarry draped by silverweed
    And lit by speedwell, where the rabbits build
Their long cool corridors, some curious seed
    Had fallen, and a leaf with edges frilled,
    As is the thistle's, grew and has now filled
Those sandy ways ; its flower a pale gold
    With purple veins, unknown to people skilled
In wild flowers' names, in flower-books untold.
Three feet its pale bells rise, a marvel to behold.

Now, white and gold, Madonna lilies shine,
    And larkspur to its fullest height has grown.
Black currants ripen, and beyond the line
        That separates the wild lands from the sown
        Ragwort begins to flash, and all alone
In shadow of the branches of a tree
        A Little Willowherb has lately blown,
And in the dark of woodlands one may see
Enchanter's nightshade gleam like a faint galaxy.

I heard last night that wild strange cry that thrills
    Through Irish fields when all is hushed and late,
And little creatures hear (and their blood chills)
        Far from their homes, and run, and meet their fate,
        The vixen's hunting-cry ; and what a spate
Of memories from that one cry are flowing
        From seasons that to sport were dedicate,
The Meath in full cry over the fields going,
Two hundred riders, most gone where there is no knowing.

22

To-day I saw the wind with silver feet
    Run over grass from which the hay was mown
Not a month since, so swiftly in the heat
        And shadows of our days the grass is grown.
        The argus butterfly has lately flown
Along our glades and, where the sun streamed through,
        Lighted with flashes from the white spots strown
Upon his dark brown wings the shadowy hue
Of the wood's ways, as on his airy dance he flew.

Now privet blooms, whose scent draws butterflies,
    And now the bramble, and along a glade
The spotted orchid stands in its full size,
        And that bright orchid of the richest shade,
        The pyramid, appears and, like green jade,
Beyond the wood the crops of wheat extend,
        And with his beard the barley is arrayed.
Shield-fern and hartstongue grow at the field's end
And all among the trees their graceful branches bend.

One of my old gnomes going for a drive
    Passed on a low cart, for they take to-day
The haycocks to their shelter, to survive
    The storms of winter in one heap of hay
    Under an iron roof. The skies are grey,
And yet from any hill a coloured view
    Spreads out to North and West and rolls away
Through pasture and land green with wheat, and through
Fields silver with young oats, to where far hills are blue.

25

And over that wide view the sunlight roams
    In wandering patches, gilding here the green,
Or touching there the roofs of little homes,
    Turning a spire white that all day had been
    A line of darkness in the distant scene.
And far away, as though another land,
    Glimmers the line of low blue hills between
The earth and sky, like fading dreams that stand
An instant, sleep and day flashing on either hand.

26

So many swallows are in air to-day
    That all the young broods must have taken wing :
White bodies with blue backs curve on their way
    With sharp wings and forked tails, and a blue ring
    Goes round their throats, under a glimmering
Of tawny brown, scarce seen as they flash by,
    However close. Again their circles swing
Low to the grass under a cloudy sky,
Foretelling further rain to all who watch them fly.

27

Half in the lazy stream and half on land
    Water-forget-me-nots in bloom have made
A wild blue garden : lower down there stand
    Flowering grasses like a palisade :
    A meadow-pea shines golden in the shade,
And one of betony's relations glows
    Under a bank beside a great green blade.
And ivy drooping from a laurel throws
A noose into the stream which there takes root and grows.

One of the ways of watching the wild lives
   That share the world with us is, in a boat,
To drift along a river, where there thrives
   The bulrush by the banks ; they scarce take note
   Of an approach that comes with things afloat,
Not with the stride for which their eyes and ears
   Watch through a life-time ; birds that were remote
Run on the mud beside one, or appears
The heron standing close, with the bright trout he spears.

29

Syringa to its fullest glory comes,
   Houndstongue is out and the mauve asters blow,
And the pink mallow. Not as yet there hums
   The bees' full chorus in the limes, although
   We hear their voices where the blossoms show,
A treasure of pale gold in the green gloom
   Of the high vaulted dome that all bees know.
Sometimes the sun shines, sometimes the clouds loom,
And Summer's heat is here and all the dahlias bloom.

30

Round, ochre patches where the haycocks were
   Show in the brilliance of surrounding green,
And peace we have not earned is in the air,
   Peace we have not deserved is o'er the scene.
   Or does this heavy silence only mean
A lack of interest in life and death
   And in that cause which for five years has been
A bright flame burning, that the angry breath
Of tyranny beats low but ne'er extinguisheth?

31

Neutrality ! It is not one to us
   Whether French workers toil in Germany
Or whether they be free. If men are thus
   To be exported into slavery
   We shall make slaves as good as what may be
In France or Holland. Buyers will come here
   And sell us, if the arms of Liberty
Do not prevail ; and, though its end is near,
The cause of slavery is still in full career.

The year moves on ; crowsfoot is going over
    And lady's-bedstraw has begun to blow.
Where hay was cut there has come back the clover,
      Crimson and white ; and, where weeds wildly grow,
      Comfrey is all in flower. Now a glow
Blushes upon the nectarines and peaches,
    And blossoms of the phlox begin to show.
Now husks are green and turning brown on beeches
And higher day by day the throttling bindweed reaches.

Veronica's small delicate white bloom
    Among its little leaves is glimmering ;
A bush of it is standing in the gloom
      Of a great cypress, where the comfreys swing
      Their purple bells ; and near them slumbering,
And dreaming of the past, some hazels stand
    (Too old for nuts) to which the lichens cling,
Giving their bit of garden an unplanned
And curious air, as of some haunted elfin land.

34

And alyssum appears, white blooms with scent
    Purely of honey ; berries are now green
On box and laurel ; and the berberis, lent
      By China to our isles, has some while been
      Heavy with berries, dark as the serene
Blue sky of midnight. Now from hedgerows peer
    The pale blue scabious, and there may be seen
Abundant yarrow. Meadowsweet is here
With tall valerian's great pink clusters rising near.

35

In cottage gardens now the rambler roses
    Show their full glory. Sometimes one may see
A garden that by old thick walls reposes
      Where none goes now, and higher than the knee
      The grass has grown, and any flowers there be
Are under the huge leaves that coltsfoot grows,
    And there cow-parsnip's white bloom crests a sea
Of deep weeds : silver-weed among them goes
Like a sea-current bright, and in the sunlight glows.

36

A field of wheat is like some blueish jade,
    Till a cloud passes and the gleaming wheat,
Acre by acre, takes a darker shade.
    Where among rushes and by meadowsweet
    A small stream runs, brooklime's bright flowers greet
The ripples' dance, bluer than turquoises.
    And where the ripples with the marshes meet
Rushes are all in bloom, and brilliancies
Of willowherb sleep still, or wake by twos and threes.

37 July 16

Pale blue I saw some distant hills to-day
    Look at our fields as from another land.
Those pale-blue distant hills, what share have they
    In planning things we thought that we had planned?
    Always beyond the fields we understand
There loomed that influence, that elfin blue,
    Luring us as though earth were but the strand
Of some immeasurable sea they knew,
Whose dreams we too should dream, whose waters travel through.

38

Much might be said of that blue world of dreams
    West of our fields, but I tell only here
Of passing days and each new flower that gleams:
    The bennet's little yellow blossoms peer,
    Stonecrop is out, the orchid lifts his spear,
The berries flush already from the thorn.
    Can they be hinting yet that Autumn's near?
A deeper colour comes into the corn.
Pale in the bright sky shows the old moon's dwindling horn.

39 July 17

Again last night the little stream asleep
    Dreamed of the bygone years when it had been
A river running with a wider sweep,
    And, like a ghost returning to the scene
    It once had known, a grey mist rose between
The woods and a low hill: blue was the sky
    As stalks of wheat that fade into jade-green;
The sun had long since set, but still on high
Was one bright scarlet cloud which drifted slowly by.

40

Now sycamore's winged seeds are turning red
    And bumble-bees below the limes are lying,
The victims of a war which overhead
    Rages each year, some dead, some slowly dying,
    As in our wars.   An old straw-stack is drying
In the hot sun, having absorbed the rain
    Of years, and sunk in little valleys vying
In greenness with the earth.   To-day with pain
And horror we have read of Aradour-sur-Glane.

41

Spiders' webs in the box are broad and deep
    And in the middle of his web there lies
The yellow spider, or enjoys a sleep
    Behind his curtains, ready to arise
    The moment any thread gives news of flies
Lost in his dreadful trap, then down he'll run
    Upon his eight sharp claws, and the small cries
Of his doomed prey will shrill.   Beneath the sun
What race or tribe is there not threatened by its Hun?

42   *July* 18

And now the water-plantain's flowers gleam
    With their three petals, where its large leaves lift
On tall stalks from the surface of a stream.
    A small round wren goes by from rift to rift
    In the green rushes by the water's drift,
Its shrill emphatic chirp arising clear.
    And now before the store-house of their thrift
The golden wasps, flash upon flash, appear
And glimmer in the shadowed home to which they steer.

43   *July* 19

Now lady's-bedstraw lights the sides of roads
    With its deep yellow, and by cottages
Budleia's branches hang their purple loads
    Which lure the wandering fritillaries,
    And willowherb is making prophecies
Of its approaching splendour, and the ears
    Of wheat are changing colour, and one sees
Cloud-mountains rising in enormous tiers
As beautiful as those that can outlast the years.

44

Now swallows meet in air as on the plate
    With willows, once designed by the Chinese.
Hydrangea climbs a garden wall where late
    Hang blooms of escallonia, and by these
    Climbs ceanothus, blue as happy seas.
On all grass pathways large black slugs abound.
    Veronica blooms thickly, and where trees
Cast a deep shadow over all the ground
Campanula in gleaming companies is found.

45   *July 20*

The mushrooms have pushed up their wild white heads
    The last few days ; and now the rambler rose
Covers the pergolas ; in flower-beds
    Goldenrod flashes, and a mullein grows,
    A wild weed of the kind that no one sows,
Among far-travelled flowers. A beech, hung
    With all the splendour of the Autumn, glows,
An Autumn of its own, like a song sung
In his last hours by a poet that died young.

46

Now the marsh-thistles bloom and their tall cousins,
    The common thistles, and the splendid flower
Of the spear-thistle shows by scores and dozens,
    For thistles now look forward to the hour,
    Told by their prophets in some secret bower,
When they shall rule the world instead of Man.
    At every Summer's end their coming power
Is prophesied afresh. Maybe they plan
More hopefully this year, while Mars helps all he can.

47   *July 21*

A large green moth is out, whose lovely wings
    Illuminate their little patch of night.
The bur-reeds have begun their flowerings,
    And loosestrife gives its shaft of coloured light
    To marshy places and to waters bright,
And in their purple splendour plums appear
    On garden walls, and now the gold and white
Of the Madonna lilies flashes clear,
But they are past their prime and feel the waning year.

Syringa too is giving up its glory.
   Blue tits and finches flit from tree to tree.
And little knowledge have we of their story
     From the rare flashes of their flight we see,
     Or from the small shrill songs that happily
Rise from their festivals, where green and gold
     Their leafy world lifts up, a world that we
Know only dimly, as we know some old
And legendary tale that is to children told.

49

The harebell, that on Surrey's sandy soil,
   Or hills of Kent or Sussex, prospers well,
Is out in gardens here, and bees despoil
     The earliest gentians now : no bluer bell
     Swings upon any stalk ; and now there swell
To their full size the evening primroses,
     Large blooms of palest gold.   For while the knell
Of thousands rings, and while catastrophes
Strike elsewhere, flowers here smile on in idle ease.

Knapweed begins to show his ruddy face
   Beside the roads.   Herb-bennet peeps through yarrows.
Willow-herb flashes.   Oats have grown apace,
     Their stalks so strong they hold the weight of sparrows.
     Low among waving weeds a streamlet narrows,
Where it goes lazily through miles of flowers
     Under old willows and by duns and barrows
And farms and cottages and ruined towers,
And whispers softly past the water-ouzel's bowers.

The corncrake to its home has come again,
   The home it fled from when they cut the hay
More than a month ago, its creaking strain
     Has sounded in our ears since yesterday.
     And in another field, on the bare clay,
A brown rectangle shows, where stood a tent
     For cricketers last year, but an array
Of sandworts and prunella now present
To that lone patch of earth its only ornament.

Now ether throbs with rumours whispering
    All is not wholly well with tyranny.
Our cause sustained us when no other thing
     Was there to help us. Has the enemy
     A cause to aid him in calamity ?
Will massacre, reprisals, torture, spies,
     Ruthlessness, gas-chambers and slavery
Uphold him with defeat before his eyes
When the vile spirit that inspires his Hitler dies ?

.   53   *July 25*

Agrimony's gold spire of blossoms gleams
    Beside the roads, and now in small dogs' hair
Its burrs appear. Now too St. John's wort beams
     With its bright face by garden paths and where
     Stand any palisades that men prepare
Against the ancient wild, whose armies are
     Thistledown, darnel, nettle, dock and tare.
The last of London-pride shines like a star
In shady places, and the cuckoo has flown far.

54   *July 26*

Where the wood-sorrel, the true shamrock, spreads
    One wide green carpet, Creeping-Jenny shows
Its bright gold flower ; and in garden beds
     The flaming dahlias now outstare the rose
     Across a path where she demurely grows
With soberer beauty ; and now heliotrope,
     Though not in the full splendour that it knows
In southern lands, blooms in a smaller scope.
And wide on a dark world still shines its brightening hope.

55

Wide on the Vistula the world's hope shines.
    But here in Ireland we watch lesser things.
Grapes are now hanging green upon our vines,
     And peaches redden. The wild strawberry swings
     Its little lantern, though the lingerings
Of its proud kin across the garden wall
     Are few indeed and scarcely lure the wings
Of the black raider with the lovely call,
Whose welcome to the dawn in April thrills us all.

Last night some travellers passed overhead
    And a few sheep cried out as they went through.
I think Neutrality was what they said.
      But an owl with more wisdom cried Who ? Who ?
      They passed, and what they were we never knew.
But our skies thrilled awhile, as though so near,
    And yet unrecognised, great spirits flew
And whispered to our fields where none would hear,
Then left us, with no Cause or splendour to revere.

57

Now sow-thistle and dandelion wait
    To launch upon the winds their wandering seeds
And find new homes beyond the garden gate,
      Behind which now they share with other weeds
      Patches of soil intended for the needs
Of statelier growths ; and outside under trees,
      Mysterious in the dusk, the toadstool breeds
And the brown puff-ball. Who is out late sees
The bat on his lone quest go fluttering through the breeze.

A black cloud-mountain lifted in the West,
    While in the East red raging clouds were rolled,
And to the left of them were peaks at rest
    In a calm light that tinted them with gold.
    So set the sun last night ; and we behold
Ever above our hills and woods and granges
    This daily wonder, past what may be told,
These airy islands whose gold outline changes
In turquoise seas asleep by ruby-crested ranges.

59

If a mad map-maker made every day
    A map of the fair mountains and the isles
He saw at sunset, what a world astray
    Beyond our boundaries, what bays and kyles
    Of faery seas, what thunder-girt defiles
Of magic mountains, were recorded then,
    Lands in which Pegasus might go for miles,
With equal ease over high crags or fen,
By destined riders steered, but by no other men.

60

To-day we heard the bells of Moscow chime,
　　Ringing across the world in ecstasy,
Two blended wonders, for what tale has Time
　　To match Marconi's, or can even he
　　Tell of a more stupendous victory
Than on that battlefield where Russians fight
　　Along a thousand miles from sea to sea
And put the arms of tyranny to flight
That Liberty may dawn on lands where all was night ?

61

To trivial things again from this high theme
　　I turn my pen, things that go quietly on
Like the slow smoke of leaf-fires from which gleam
　　Bright fires but rarely, their vermilion
　　Glowing a moment, then where they have shone
Draws in the Autumn night ; so these great deeds
　　Flash out amid the ages and are gone,
And the calm growing of a myriad seeds
In peaceful fields is all, awhile, that History heeds.

62

Now where the bean-rows thrive in lowliness,
　　Far from the prouder roses, shines the flame
Of scarlet runners, like a gorgeous dress
　　Upon a working man.　As though it came
　　Of its own will to visit kindred, tame
In flower-beds, there blooms the camomile
　　Near gardens, but on land they do not claim.
In their full glory now snapdragons smile,
And dahlias and sweet-peas gleam with them for a while.

63　　　　　　　　　　　　*July 29*

A second brood of swallows may be seen,
　　Some on the nest's edge, some aloft in air
Not far from windows where their homes have been,
　　With flight all new to them and strange and rare,
　　Though very soon they will all further fare
Than most of us, when warmth goes and they follow,
　　To where the oleanders bloom and where
The cork-woods sleep, and in some leafy hollow
They will find sunlight still and shelter, every swallow.

31

C

64   *July* 30

Now the gay rosettes of the hollyhocks
    Begin to show where the last lupins die,
And summer by the dandelions' clocks
    Is past its noon. So low the swallows fly,
    They nearly touch the grass ; a heavy sky
Unites with them in prophesying rain.
    A trifling theme, the rain, yet history
Is often shaped by it, and man in vain
Seeks to escape the lot that sun and storm ordain.

65   *July* 31

The foxtongue fern is hanging out from walls,
    And the day-lily shows its shining head.
Sometimes the coloured snail along it crawls,
    Near to the top ; and now the fiery red
    Of the montbretia lights a flowerbed.
How far this month, across how many streams,
    Has Liberty advanced ! Her armies tread
By German borders, and at last it seems
The world may soon awake from Hitler's frightful dreams.

AUGUST

August is come, the month from which the world
    Expects so much.   But here the world goes by
And leaves us, as it leaves the meteors hurled
    Beyond its course in the November sky,
    And Ireland watches dandelions die
And apples ripen and the crops grow brown
    And the fritillaries to flowers fly,
And bumble-bees begin to settle down
In the blue thistle which wears now its azure crown.

2

And tortoiseshells are flying to the flowers,
    And daily lovelier are hollyhocks
And gladiolus lights the sunny hours,
    And asters have begun to gleam, and stocks,
    And a stale scent arises from the phlox,
And wasps are everywhere and cinquefoils creep
    Over the paths, and seeds are on the docks,
And large moths sail when birds no longer cheep,
And on the scabious now the burnet lies asleep.

3

Now on the red bogs bell-heather and ling
    Begin to bloom : wild lanes from tended land
Run down to them, where the great-bindweeds cling
    To hedges, and green fronds of bracken stand ;
    And the lanes end, and suddenly expand
Those strange brown acres shaking to the tread,
    Lit by rose-willow, where a little band
Cuts turf in small rectangles, harvested .
In stacks like hay, and white bog-cotton waves its head.

4

Some seedling birches roam a little way
    Into the bog and cease, a swallow flies
As though it wondered who had dared to stray
    Into this wilderness, where sphagnum lies
    By deep brown pools and the bog-myrtles rise,
And the bog-asphodel like fairy gold,
    And human footsteps come as a surprise,
And all is as it has been from of old,
And over it unchanged a thousand years have rolled.

5

Only in deepest pools the moss is wet
    In August ; elsewhere it is white and dry.
But under steep brown banks its colours yet
    Flash as in Winter, and strange landscapes lie
    Fashioned in moss, where mountains two feet high
Rise from a green plain decked with little flowers
    Beside a small lake mirroring the sky,
A group of kingdoms ruled by fairy powers.
And the turf-cutters' bank sheer over them all towers.

6

Near the bog's edge the yellow-loosestrife teems
    In fields but lately won from moss and ling,
And there the celandine all golden gleams.
    And now the bog is gone and gardens cling
    To solid earth, for never wandering
Far from the homes of men goes celandine.
    And eyebright twinkles, and that lovely thing
The scented orchid rises, and there shine
Blue vetches in the hedge, through which their tendrils twine.

7

August 3

Dark red carnations with their scent of cloves,
    And scarlet ones, and yellow ones and white,
In open air bloom now where the bee roves,
    And Japanese anemones are bright
    As graceful ghosts upon a Summer's night.
The pergola with all its weight of roses
    Still shines by cypresses, but past the height
Of its full beauty, and now tired reposes
The honeysuckle's bloom as its long season closes.

8

The name of hyacinthus candidans
　　Conceals a flower lovelier than its name :
The long description is some learned man's ;
　　But still some distant land from which it came,
　　Like a trapped eagle that will not be tame,
It seems remembering ; its graceful bells,
　　Swinging and gleaming, silently proclaim
Their origin in far and faery dells,
Where music none of ours in magic cadence swells.

9

Thirty years since were many vain words said
　　And many false hopes dreamed of ending war,
And Ares laughed to hear that he was dead
　　When his four years of massacre were o'er !
　　How wise we were ! There should be war no more :
Nations should vote against it. And what man
　　Would dare to draw sword, or what cannon roar,
Against the votes of Finns, Irak, Iran,
Portugal, Panama, Spain, Iceland and Japan ?

10　　　　　　　　　　　　*August* 4

The white bloom of the polyanthus rose
　　Attracts a butterfly as white as it,
Which swoops down for a moment and then goes,
　　As though it were its kin and thought it fit
　　To wave its recognition. Now there sit
On the blue thistle, a round mass of bloom,
　　Bumblebees, and fritillaries all lit
With sunlight, even when the sun in gloom
Of passing clouds is hid and shadows, elsewhere, loom.

11

There lies a thick grey mist which no wind steers.
　　One could imagine Destiny to-day
Let down a curtain after thirty years
　　Upon a scene now ended, in a play
　　We think we understand ; but what there may
Come in the next scene cannot be foretold.
　　For like blind men on unknown shores astray
We plan, and soon along the bays are rolled
By fated tides too strong for our poor dykes to hold.

Last night the full moon like a disc of gold
　　Shone on the mist, but did not light the trees,
Whose figures rose enormous, dark and old,
　　　And did not stir a leaf in any breeze ;
　　　And silence lay as heavy as deep seas ;
And through the fields from very far the bark
　　　Of one dog broke upon the mysteries
Of the deep night and thrilled them, as a spark
May give intensity to the surrounding dark.

13

Berries of mountain ash are turning red,
　　And red are berries of the Austrian rose.
The last anemone now droops its head,
　　　Having survived the company of those
　　　That bloom all April, exiles that repose
Far from the isles that they and Victory
　　　Had loved so long, the land that glory knows,
Whose smiles are mirrored in a sapphire sea,
Greece, for a little while in dreadful slavery.

14　　　　　　　　*August* 6

The spider working all along a hedge
　　Has caught the morning mist ; his hammocks lie
Draped with white sheets of it ; by the road's edge
　　　The burdock has begun to bloom, and high
　　　The woody nightshade climbs ; a butterfly
Haunts every cottage garden ; the bees' song
　　　Is ended in the limes.　Through a calm sky
The moon rode red last night, then gold, and long
Gazed at earth, as though here peace never suffered wrong.

15

A thunderstorm went by with sheets of rain
　　And left a few clouds caught in a high wood.
In all the trees its echoes still remain,
　　　And in their branches you can hear a flood.
　　　Along the paths, marked out in sandy mud,
Are maps of rivers.　Earth is cloaked in grey
　　　And sleeps, and you can feel her gratitude
For this great shower that has fallen to-day
And with the thunder trailed its long white skirts away.

Ivy-leaf toadflax with its violet hue
    Rambles upon long tendrils on the stone
Of an old arch that nobody goes through.
    And now the airy dragonflies have flown
    Out of their hidden haunts.   An art was known
Among them for a thousand centuries,
    Which we have copied. Were it let alone
Had it been better ?   But what prophet sees
Where we are swept along by our discoveries ?

17

A burning-bush, that leans over a lawn
    Beside an ilex, has begun to glow.
The gleam of it is like a misty dawn,
    Or sunset during thunder.   Now there show
    The berries of the guelder-rose, whose snow
Has long since melted in the glare of Time.
    Their scarlet flashes and, beyond, arow
The roses still along the trellis climb,
But fading now; and dead are blossoms of the lime.

18

The air is now like some caerulean sea
    Sailed by explorers in the days of Drake,
But not for man : the dragonfly and bee,
    The wasp and fly, their many journeys make ;
    Now is their season, and their myriads wake.
As Spaniards set out for Pacific beaches,
    So wasps set sail in air for plunder's sake.
Now ripen, as we think for us, the peaches,
But none of them beyond these bright adventurers' reaches.

19   *August* 8

Yesterday there swept over us a shower
    Suddenly, and before the rain was gone
The sun came out in all his golden power.
    One beech-tree, as though touched by magic, shone
    In bands of azure, green, vermilion,
Transmuted by a rainbow : such a light
    Touches our earth but rarely. Sailing on
Against a thundercloud as black as night
A swallow flew. One scarce knew swallows were so white.

20

Still shine the sunny marigolds : all June,
    And all July, they gave their radiant glow
To cheer the garden, which will lose them soon ;
      Like quantities of suns, such as may flow
      Along the Milky Way, their faces show ;
A merry company, a golden band,
    That need no way to Eldorado know :
They are themselves all gold, and there's no land
They would not make more bright by sailing to its strand.

21   *August* 9

The wonderful cascade of traveller's joy
    Begins to bloom ; patches of flowers shine
Upon its summits, where they most enjoy
      The sunlight, as foam touches the long line
      Of a green wave ; as high as beech or pine
Can soar it clambers, and from there descends
    In the green torrent of its steep decline.
No tree has beauty such as this plant lends,
But trees it so enchants are drawing near their ends.

22   *August* 10

The jade-green berries of the laurel burn
    To red and purple where they get the sun.
Crimson the nectarines and peaches turn,
      And a few grapes get colour one by one :
      And now the time of gooseberries is done.
Moths on their rapid journeys pass one by.
    Budleia's purple blooms still prosper, none
Without the glow of its fritillary
Or the bright wandering wings of the white butterfly.

23

The moon is ageing. What will it behold
    Before it comes round to the full once more ?
But if the moon cares aught for what is told
      Of our Earth's story, it will watch the shore
      Of ocean, or some river's tidal bore,
Rather than heed the raging tides of man,
    Though these as loudly as the others roar.
For human bloodshed flows beyond the plan
That either moon or we have ever made, or can.

The lime-blossom is brown upon the ground,
    Each blossom winged, but with a single wing ;
Acorns begin to grow on oaks, and round
    Are chestnuts in their husks, and withering
    Are fallen walnuts, though the ones that swing
Upon the tree are still unripe and green.
    Plums are all lovely shades, some ripening,
Some yellow, green or pink. Now the serene
Ageing of Summer, with last gifts of fruit is seen.

Down a long valley that through pastures weaves
    The Boyne below its silver willows sweeps,
And wild ducks hide among the iris leaves,
    And rocks show now in what were lately deeps,
    And here and there a swan swims by, or sleeps.
How like a river is to Time, who stays
    For nothing beautiful, but onward keeps
Towards whatever deep beyond our days
Draws all Creation's stars upon their unknown ways.

And near the Boyne a quarry of grey sand,
    Borne by old rivers, shows on its dry wall
The currents that had swept along a strand
    Gone before earliest memorial
    That man has made ; and there sand-martins call
One to the other as they sail in air
    Above their many doorways dark and small
In the steep cliff the quarrymen laid bare,
Which houses now their broods in such abundance there.

Snowberries now begin to flash from hedges
    And flax is blooming, blue as brightest sky ;
Convolvulus has climbed over the edges
    Of garden walls and peers at passers-by
    With its triumphant head uplifted high.
And robin-run-the-hedge, at war with man,
    Moves in from the free land to occupy
Whatever tame and tended fields it can
And dreams of weedy wastes which the wild green things plan.

28

Two months have passed since I began this rhyme,
  And Earth a sixth part of her course has run,
And Liberty has marched on all the time
    Out of the night and looks upon the sun,
    A march we see not here, and so begun
This poem was, to tell of lesser things.
    Yet I remember, ere her cause was won,
How weak in Greece appeared her drooping wings
And how in Kent the foe mocked at their flutterings.

August 14

29

Marjoram blossoms by the sides of ways,
  Lured out by sunlight that has brought far hills
Clear into view; and in these shining days
    The bloom of red geraniums often fills
    Green boxes upon cottage window-sills.
And now the peacock butterfly appears
    In crimson splendour, and the whole world's ills
Are something that the reaper dimly hears,
For there have passed us by the world's five greatest years ;

30

Hard, hard enough, but from them History
  Refines her gold in furnace of our day,
Which burns up monument and pageantry,
    Leaving the things that cannon cannot slay
    And memories that will not pass away,
Endurances and darings that have saved
    The world from worse than any man can say,
The horror of a continent enslaved
And for the world such laws as Hitler might have raved.

August 15

31

The gladioli share the garden now
  With hollyhocks and snapdragons and roses,
And apples are in clusters on the bough ;
    And now the aster his deep shade discloses,
    And still the dahlia, till the sun reposes,
Flashes and twinkles with the Summer's gold :
    The well-fed wasp upon the ripe pear dozes,
And all the bright sweet-peas are growing old,
And waves of brown ripe wheat across the fields are rolled.

32

To-day I saw a thistledown blow by.
    How great our aims ! What mighty plans our theme !
How carefully we chart futurity !
    Haply the thistledown has, too, its dream.
    And the wind blows and the white speck agleam
Drifts with it. Can we stop war for a day,
    When it would come, by any careful scheme ?
Or do we, like the thistle, drift away
On some eternal blast that heeds no words we say ?

33

And not into destruction drifts the seed,
    But, where the wind may bear it, blooms once more.
Nor does war's wrath destroy the human breed,
    But moves it up and down from shore to shore,
    And grimly writes our histories in gore
And builds our boundaries ; that ancient curse
    Has been throughout our era, and before,
Guiding our steps for better as for worse.
Alas ! Let us be told. Bellona was our nurse.

34

How quiet it is here ! But four years ago
    Over our roof in Kent the world was saved,
For Hitler swore upon that day to show
    His face in London; and there never waved
    The swastika above our land enslaved,
Because the Air Force turned him back that day
    And many more. Away that dream has raved
Among old nightmares and is far away,
But we and all men then were nearly Hitler's prey.

35   *August* 16

Young wild duck now are strong upon the wing,
    And where they swim the water-speedwell grows
With all its little flowers blossoming,
    And there the water-mint abundant blows,
    With round mauve blooms upon the stalk in rows,
And arrowhead's three petals may be found,
    Rising on tall stems where deep water flows,
And all beside it willowherbs abound,
And wind in reeds and trees is there the only sound. ·

36

36 August 17

The honeysuckle's berries have turned red,
    And reddening are berries of the thorn ;
The blossom of the blackberry is dead,
    And red and green and brown its fruits adorn
    The roadside hedge, and brown is all the corn.
Still low among tall reeds Boyne slowly runs.
    But all our thoughts are now upon the Orne,
Or with the Americans at Chartres, whose guns'
Prophetic voice is heard in Paris by the Huns.

37 August 18

Swallows in greater numbers crowd the air,
    As though already they foresaw the day
When they will soar to those bright spaces where
    The North wind that will take them on their way
    Is waiting for them ; for, like men, they sway
About the world, the swallows at known times,
    Men unpredicted in the times they stray.
Yet, sure as swallows, into other climes
Their armies move, to make our histories and rhymes.

38

Now helianthus, as gaillardia dies,
    Shines in the garden : catmint droops its head :
To-day under damp, warm and heavy skies
    The first chrysanthemums appear, and red
    Glows the montbretia, like to thin flames spread
Out from a camp-fire by the falling weight
    Of the last log a hunter throws ere bed,
To scare the lions. As the year grows late
Michaelmas daisies peer through leaves, but hesitate.

39

Now, like the hills and valleys of a land
    More flowery than any that we know,
Blooms the wild clematis, whose rope-like strand
    Climbs to a tree-top, whence its splendours flow
    Through green ravines to widening vales below,
Sparkling with starry flowers. Now the air
    Rings suddenly with victory, as though
A sword had struck an ogre to the hair
Through his gross helm, as he ate men's flesh in his lair.

And liberated belfries, now, in France
    Ring to the ether, and the Marseillaise
Is heard again, and news of our advance
    Tells even of Versailles. In darker days
    We found hope easy ; now its brilliant rays
Flash from outside us, and our country needs
    Our hope no more, though once such slender stays
Seemed all she had. Here softly grow the weeds
And neutrals smoke their pipes, and cattle graze the meads.

41 *August* 19

This is a day, from any hill-top seen,
    In which far mountains seem to float in air ;
And counties lie in sunlight, gold and green,
    Though one or two lie dark in shadow where
    A stray cloud wanders ; light smoke here and there
Drifts on a slow wind, or a far spire gleams.
    To show that mankind has some little share
In the vast scene, which to the westward seems
To lie along the dim blue borderland of dreams.

42

I saw the rooks fly slowly home to-night,
    Calling to one another on their way,
As calm, as leisurely in their long flight
    As though no trouble shook the world to-day.
    And what is war to them or rapine ? They
Take their old journey. They know when men sow,
    And when they reap the corn, and when they slay.
They are such ancient neighbours that they know
More than we ever guess about the way we go.

43 *August* 20

Now in our garden in its splendour glows
    Lobelia cardinalis : such a red
A cardinal might envy, or the rose.
    And now symphyndra lifts its fiery head
    Ten foot in air above a potting shed.
And still the bright snapdragons hold their own
    Against whatever rumour flowers dread,
When some cold breeze along the paths has blown
Hinting that even the rose may soon be overthrown.

44

Lavender's little bloom begins to fade,
    But its scent lingers as a memory
May linger of a good life, when the shade
    Of earth is on the bones eternally.
    Full of sweet scents are gardens ; rosemary
Grows there with its thin odorous leaves, dark green
    Above and white below, and there may be
Patches of mint, and thyme's mauve bloom is seen,
Which scents the Kentish hills and all the vales between.

45

To-day a cold wind sets the trees astir
    As though a breath of Autumn touched the cheek
Of Summer as she said farewell to her.
    The land lies shadowed, and the air is bleak.
    Far to the West from Tara lies a streak
Of light, beyond which hills seem strange and bright
    These are the hills the old kings used to seek
Who died at Tara ; under that dim light
They lie on the low slopes that gleam in Tara's sight.

46

And now rain falls, as though the Summer wept
    At parting, for she will leave Ireland soon,
And with her all the swallows will be swept.
    She will go South by light of next full moon,
    Where Andalusia seems an endless June ;
Over its oleanders drifting she
    Will fly to Africa, and hear the tune
The Arabs play when touched by phantasy,
Where the Sahara laps the mountains like a sea.

47

Paris is free ! Paris is free at last !
    Through four years she endured the arrogance
Of a gross conqueror, and those years are past.
    The lovely city from its dire mischance
    Emerges, as at dawn when sunrays glance,
After a night of thunder, on her spires,
    And she is queen of a triumphant France,
On which a shadow still glooms, but retires,
Drifting towards the Rhine with smoke of dreadful fires.

48

And still the news pours in, news of a world
    Waking to liberty from evil dreams,
Eastward away with all their phantoms hurled,
    And a new morning upon Europe gleams.
    Shall we be worthy of the day that seems
So full of golden hope, or shall we sink
    Back among cocktails, sloth and petty themes?
Yet there has come new wisdom, as I think,
To all of us who stood upon disaster's brink.

49   *August 24*

Last night Rumania left the robber band,
    Rumania so much loved by her fair Queen,
Who died before she saw her luckless land
    Dragged upon an adventure that has been
    The costliest failure that the world has seen,
Paid for with bones that from the Caucasus
    To Bessarabia birds have long picked clean.
Now in the sight, at last, of all of us
The fortress of our foe stands cracked and ruinous.

50   *August 25*

Still through our garden Summer glides away,
    And bindweed climbs, although a world is breaking,
And wasps fly to the plums, though every day
    A page of some tremendous tale is making
    And millions are in arms and kingdoms quaking.
Still butterflies draw honey deep from flowers,
    As though all Man has builded were not shaking,
As though the agony of evil powers
Cast no fair cities down in their last frantic hours.

51

And faint as footfall of a ghost appear
    Stray hints of Autumn; even now the vines
Under their glass have heard that she is near;
    The grapes are turning blue, and crimson twines
    With green along the leaves; now brightly shines
The mountain-ash with berries, and the snails
    Begin to climb, and hips and haws in lines
Redden, and hazel-nuts in sunny vales
Glow pink, and over them the large red-admiral sails.

Willows are turning silver more and more
    And just the very faintest touch of gold
Is mixing with the silver, where there pour
      The waters of the Boyne, whose high banks hold
      Gardens by homes, and ruins manifold,
Which seem the chief antagonists of Time,
    Though the thick rushes were already old
And rooted firmly in the river's slime
Ere any ruin's bells had uttered their first chime.

The swallows up and down by windows glide
    In hurried curves through rainy air and gray,
As though their little minds were occupied
      With some impending destiny which they
      Feel in their hearts, as Man might feel to-day.
The ether throbs for us with those events
    That shake our age, as all the winds that stray
Are warning swallows of their banishments,
Soon to see stormy tides, and then the Arabs' tents.

No stranger magic did Sir Walter Scott
    Ever imagine of the chiming bells
Of Notre Dame, charmed from afar, than what
      We hear to-day, the wakened chime that tells
      Paris is free, and through the ether swells
To cheer all men that worship Liberty.
    We heard it here, the chime that surely knells
The doom of massacre and tyranny,
Piercing this lifeless gloom we call Neutrality.

The meadow-peas, clutching at blades of grass
    With little tendrils, smile amongst the green
With golden faces ; and the splendours pass
      From gardens, where brown gaps are to be seen
      Among the snapdragons, which earthward lean ;
And over are the lilies, and an eerie
    Omen of Autumn troubles the serene
Of sunset, and the dahlias seem weary,
The hollyhocks alone upstanding tall and cheery.

A dwarf chrysanthemum puts out its flowers,
    And gold with wasps is every fallen pear,
And round the grapes through all the sunny hours
    Their golden cohorts murmur in the air.
    Crimson the stalks of elderberries flare.
And now soft berries of the Irish yew
    Are reddening, as titmice are aware,
That flit to gather them while ripe and new,
Singing their tiny song heard only by a few.

A touch of green is shining on the heads
    Of this year's mallards.   Swallows are still here,
Crowding about our roof, as though the leads
    Some harbour were from which they mean to steer
    On their long journey.   In the fields appear
The tapestries of spiders on the grass
    Shining with dew until the noon is near.
Sometimes swift moths over the tree-tops pass.
And numberless flies buzz on every pane of glass.

And spiders' nests, grey towers, may be seen,
    Built upon weeds and grass, and rising tall,
Gossamer palaces a fairy queen
    Might grace with tiny ceremonial,
    Ruling a population brown and small.
Now from the orchard where the full bough bends
    Goes Summer southwards at the white owl's call,
Over a sea of mist that autumn sends.
And August that has done so much for freedom ends.

SEPTEMBER

1

Yesterday thunder came and spoiled the plan
　　Of harvest, and the oats are rain-immerst.
Earthquake, volcano, hurricane and man,
　　Of all these four destroyers man is first.
　　How feeble is the lightning at its worst !
Two minutes of artillery can bring
　　A desolation that seems more accurst,
With houses staring lost and sorrowing,
Than any storm can do with all its thundering.

2

Pale gold above an oak while bats were flying
　　The moon appeared last night to light September,
And now September's here and Summer's dying.
　　This is a month the ages will remember.
　　Many a house will be a smoking ember,
Many a city will be dust and clay,
　　But Liberty will live, and when November
Comes round again with its eleventh day
There will have come that end for which free peoples pray.

3

The Autumn crocus opens now its flowers,
　　Bright mauve amongst the grass : a fairy strayed
Out of its kingdom to these fields of ours
　　Might look so lost : this flower seems arrayed
　　For early Spring, and should not see the shade
Of dying Summer ; a lost season seems
　　To shine a moment down the little glade,
As light on the late flower palely gleams,
And Spring seems somewhere near, with all her songs and dreams.

48

4

To-day amidst the news that thrills the world
   A German spoke to me, and in a tone
That angels may use, sitting with wings furled
   In calm we know not, out beyond the zone
   Of all the weary planets : one alone
Can speak thus, and his voice can reach us still,
   A spirit reigning on a lonely throne
High above all the passing ages set ;
And there Beethoven speaks as from a parapet.

5

Hypericum, or tutsan, by the road
   Shines under Tara, in its later days,
For many of its blooms feel Autumn bode
   And its red berries glitter in the rays.
   The world seems spread from Tara, girt with haze ;
And beyond that, as though another star
   Rode close beside us through the empty ways,
Blue mountains, paler than the known lands are,
Lift their enchanted heads to watch us from afar.

6   *September 3*

Last night the moon was full, gold at its rising
   And later silver, when its radiance bright
Gave shadows to the oaks almost surprising,
   As though some magic were abroad that night.
   This is the harvest moon, and by its light
In European cornfields there will be
   Things done from which the times beyond our sight
Will gather harvest of their history,
Reaped from the fields that lie bare to calamity.

7

Five years ago a ravaged world, unscarred,
   But with its follies in its midst, was hurled
By them into that maelstrom where ill-starred
   And unknown currents by the Norns are swirled.
   For five years by those streams have we been whirled,
For long through darkness, and to light at last,
   Which breaks, though stormily, upon the world,
And underneath a sky still overcast
Dim signs are seen that say the agony is past.

8

Now where the harvest is in sheaves arow,
    And some uncut, some beaten down by rain,
The crab-apples like elfin orchards glow,
    And partridges pick up the fallen grain,
    And here and there a mushroom may remain.
But sudden news has thrilled a morning hour :
    Belgium's fair capital is free again !
Eastward the armies of the tyrant lour.
Glory to England's arms ! Glory to Eisenhower !

9
September 5

I meant to tell of birds and crops and flowers,
    And little things that change upon earth's way.
But earth is passing through tremendous hours,
    And ether throbs with news that lifts my lay
    To heights on which it had not thought to stray.
Last night we heard the anthem of the Dutch
    Ringing to utter more than words could say,
And heard a Belgian speak : his joy was such
As only comes to those who lately suffered much.

10

And now the rather solemn church-like air
    Of Luxemburg along the ether goes,
For the free armies bring back freedom there,
    Where the Moselle through shining acres flows
    And mile on mile the rye all silver glows,
Where twenty-five years since I saw the smile
    Of Luxemburg to Liberty, when foes
Of this same breed had parted them awhile,
Whom free, victorious men again shall reconcile.

11
September 6

Last night twixt cloud and moon we heard go by
    Some heavy planes and wondered could there be
A wounded ally, sleeping in the sky,
    Going to cross the bleakness of the sea
    That lies beyond our bleak neutrality,
To come with morning to his native shore
    And see the statue there of Liberty,
Whose lost realm he had suffered to restore,
Whom he had helped to bring to Brittany once more.

12

Again Beethoven.   Strange that exaltations
   That make men equal to the mountains hoary
Should turn to music and to devastations ;
   Neither to be despised, for Earth's old story
   Without the arts were something transitory,
Or, spared the terrible delight of Mars,
   Earth would go wearily without her glory,
Lacking the brightness that the other stars
Have gathered to themselves from flames of unknown wars.

13 *September* 7

Cotoneaster's berries are bright red
   And the sea-buckthorn's have an orange glow.
Michaelmas daisies light a flower-bed
   With their young faces where the others strow
   Their petals, beaten by the dreary flow
Of rain that lately darkened every day,
   And even the wasps appear to fly more slow,
And hollyhocks are sere, though dahlias stay,
And Autumn walks the paths, with frost not far away.

14

Hundreds of swallows round our windows flew
   All yesterday : this morning they are gone
Upon a rainy wind, all but a few.
   Too palely for them our September shone.
   They and the wind that takes them travel on
Southward to lands that I would see again,
   Sailing perhaps to Cannes, past Avignon ;
Then the blue sea, and onward over Spain.
But these are dreams, while they see all these places plain.

15 *September* 8

Sheep-scabious beside the roads is growing,
   And all the hedges are ablaze with haws ;
A single chestnut is already showing
   To the green trees the fashion which the laws
   Of Autumn soon decree ; like sheets of gauze
Fine rain is falling ; deep blue are the sloes ;
   From old high walls comes chatter of the daws ;
In some small garden a red salvia grows
And all the rest is weeds where this one splendour glows.

16

A lake that still remembers the old place
    In which it dwelt ere cultivation came
Has stolen back and now it grows apace,
    And sea-gulls come and shine against the flame
    Of stormy sunset.   Now reports proclaim
Bulgaria makes war on Germany,
    And the hope rises that the land of fame,
Among her isles in the Aegean sea,
Will soon be once again victorious and free.

17   *September* 9

And now the lake that visited our day
    From bygone ages turns to them again
And softly from our pastures steals away,
    And sun is on the grass instead of rain ;
    And sheaves are standing in the fields of grain,
And pimpernels are gleaming in clear light,
    And heartsease now can see the heavens plain,
Which lately the corn shadowed, and the bright
Small face of speedwell shines.   And Europe turns from night.

18   *September* 10

Snakeweed and stitchwort, tare and betony,
    Are in the fields where the potatoes grow,
And fumitory blooms abundantly ;
    And now a colder wind begins to blow,
    And blackberries are ripe, and Autumn's glow
Increases in a chestnut here and there,
    And flitting to the wayside flowers go
Small butterflies, as azure as the air
Vaulted above us, which the swallows have left bare.

19

For our last swallows left us in the night,
    To follow those that went three days before
Across a troubled world, if fights men fight
    Mean aught to them : maybe the smoke and roar
    Of Man's invasions mean to them no more,
Ebbing and flowing through the centuries,
    Than means to us the flight from a far shore
Of swallows that come here to eat our flies
And, having preyed on them, pass to new destinies.

But how could anyone compare proud Man,
    Mighty and mountain-shaking as he is,
With the poor swallow, whose untutored plan
    With no regard to books or theories,
    And blindly guided by the vagaries
Of winds, or what ? . . . Ah, if one only knew
    What lore it is that guides his odysseys,
One might more easily compare the two
And give each wanderer through these dark nights his due.

21   September 11

Now the first bunches of the grapes are ripe,
    And elderberries flash beside the ways,
Black clusters on red stalks ; and, where the snipe
    Dwells in his valleys, a grey world of haze
    Shines in the evening under slanting rays
Right to a wood that rises over it
    All dark, for not as yet the wood obeys
The rule for Autumn, though the fields are lit
With its late flowers, and though all the swallows flit.

22

Yet the last swallows have not left our eaves,
    For some turned back, or lingered when the rest
Passed over the brown fields where stand the sheaves,
    And the green pastures and those hills the West
    Robes in its azure : still about the nest
They knew in Summer sail these few, their cries
    Shrilling in calm air, giving a faint zest
To the cold spaces of the Autumn skies,
Piercing a garden's hush, where the snapdragon dies.

23   September 12

Fallen by now are the potato's flowers
    In weedy fields, though still their leaves are green ;
Blue shine the turnips, making shady bowers
    For partridges, when they no longer glean
    The stubble, and the rays of evening lean
Over the land. Now wasps are crawling slow
    In houses and the blow-fly may be seen ;
And woolly-bears over the pathways go,
One day to all the pride of tiger-moths to grow.

Now red-hot-pokers in small gardens shine,
   And bright begonias and goldenrod,
And the last marigolds, with which a shrine
    Is often brightened for an Indian god.
    And surely, if the earth were ever trod
By spirits, from a stream of suns astray,
   No flowers more sunny could adorn the sod
Of Earth than these, that seem to light the day
As with a glow of suns seen very far away.

25 September 13

And sometimes berries of the guelder rose
   Flash from a hedge, outshining every flower,
A glittering scarlet.   Lines of swallows pose
    Along a railway.   In an aged tower
    A white veronica has made its bower
In a worn crevice scooped for it by Time,
   Where it is nourished by the passing shower,
And one branch blossomed there, though past its prime,
And shone in the high home to which it dared to climb.

26 September 14

And now a quarter of the year is gone
   Since at midsummer I began this lay,
And faded now are all the flowers that shone
    Whether in gardens or in fields of hay,
    Save one or two ; and, while day followed day
So uneventfully across our fields,
   Liberty marched on her tremendous way,
Scattering splendours over many wealds,
That shall surpass, when gleaned, all other ages' yields.

27

Cotoneaster, like red draperies,
   More fruit than foliage, leans on a wall,
And coral berries of a berberis
    Shine near the leaves of one that seems a fall
    Of fountains running blood ; under a pall
Of rainy skies a chestnut rattles down,
   Shining inside its husk, a polished ball
Of old mahogany all glossy brown.
And on old pasture-lands ill-suited corn-crops drown.

And last night Autumn lightly touched the trees,
  As an enchanter with his wand might touch,
Merely for practice, some base ore he sees
  Lying at hand, though not yet caring much
  To turn it into gold, by magic such
As once was studied in Valladolid
  And Salamanca, leaning on his crutch,
Day-dreaming of his mysteries, still hid
From common eyes, but soon to flash as he has bid.

29

Like a lamp lit for these Autumnal days
  The Autumn crocus glimmers in the grass.
A multitude of swallows in a maze
  Of curves and circles comes again, to pass
  Backwards and forwards by the very glass
Of every window, nimbly hunting flies
  That at this season shelter in the mass
Of ivy on old walls, and with keen eyes
Detected where they lurk, and snapped up when they rise.

30

A thuja turns half ochre and half green,
  As Autumn sets its wealth of seeds alight ;
And little shrubs, that have already seen
  The coming change, tell of it in the night
  To the tall trees that have not had the sight,
And dress themselves already to receive
  The splendid season and to greet aright
This stranger to our fields that will bereave
The rose and gild the pear and fire the skies at eve.

31   *September* 16

Now wasps are weary as they eat the grapes,
  And to the willows comes a touch of gold,
Whose leaves were green, then silver ; now the shapes
  Of gilded twigs shine through them ; and behold
  The apples' hearty blush, though growing old
Is all the garden.   Gone is every wing
  That flashed about our windows, while there rolled
The North wind up to them, now wandering
The way their fellows went, to unknown haunts of Spring.

Potatoes, turnips, stubble and red clover,
    With crops and pasture, share the countryside.
To-night I saw the rooks go calmly over
    In the vast calm of spaces deep and wide :
    Their simple destiny appeared to guide
Each wandering wing to its accustomed tree,
    A destiny unnoticed by the pride
Of our inventions. How less surely we
Move with uncertain aim to ends we cannot see.

            33   *September* 17

No leaf as yet has turned to brown or gold
    On ash-trees, but the yellow seeds appear
Among the leaves of some, while others hold
    Still the old pods that linger from last year,
    Rustling among the green leaves grey and sere.
A mighty ivy looms above a thorn,
    Like a huge tiger sprung upon a deer,
The berries flashing in the sunny morn
Under the ivy's mass. And rooks are gleaning corn.

            34   *September* 18

Now Autumn calls to spirits of the streams
    And from their valleys they arise and follow,
Vast as the estuaries of their dreams,
    Grey over green fields where the cattle wallow :
    A ghostly arm moves all along a hollow,
And after it a grey and ghostly flood,
    Chilling the corncrake, warning the last swallow.
Now stags in Scotland roar, and now a mood
Of roving brings its thrill to any wanderer's blood.

            35   *September* 19

The beeches that have seen the chestnuts change
    Try the new fashion one by one to-day,
As though each slipped an arm into the strange
    New gleaming garment but a little way
    And round their wrists allowed the bright display
To dazzle for a moment, while they showed
    To one another what fair splendours lay
Soft on their hands, and how the treasure glowed
With which for their delight so far the North wind rode,

Over the woods to-day move sun and shadow,
  And tips of trees are brighter to behold,
As though they were some folk of El Dorado
    Standing upon their frontier, taking hold
    Carelessly of small particles of gold,
While a faint glimmer from their inner land
    Stealing among them hinted more than told
Of the bright wealth that glittered in their sand,
Or flashed from golden cliffs, or heaped some river's strand.

37

The leaves and berries of a berberis glow
  Together as though burning with one fire :
Dark purple berries on another grow
    Where a thin branch sends up a scarlet spire.
    And, as the hollyhock begins to tire
And the carnation hangs her weary head,
    This plant from the World's end erects a pyre,
Which flames where Summer's blooms are lying dead
And petals of the rose on passing winds are shed.

And now a sycamore has joined the band
  Of trees that deck themselves in Autumn's dress.
In furbelows of gold she seems to stand,
    Her green frock brightened by the gaudiness,
    And, straying on her shoulder, a brown tress
Blown by the North wind shows against the green.
    They stand there waiting as for some excess
Of revelry which Autumn shall convene
When, walking with the wind, white frost shall grace the scene.

39

And one elm dresses wholly in old gold,
  As though of all the trees she only bought
With fairy coin the dress that dryads sold,
    Which they across the fields at midnight brought,
    The bright new fashion that the branches sought,
Stretching their arms for them while sunset glared
    And seemed to promise glories strangely fraught
With colours such as had not flamed and flared
Since Earth had gone once round the path on which she fared.

A robin glowing in an apple-tree
   Sang a short ditty to the setting sun,
And clustered apples glowed as well as he,
     And the last marigolds, where one by one
     Asters and pansies knew their day was done
And titmice flitted, and from far away
   A pigeon uttered such content as none
Can hark to without wonder in a day
When such disaster reigns and Hitler yet holds sway.

         September 22

A path has turned to gold under a lime,
   Whose leaves are green, and all the gold ones fell,
Torn by the equinox, which at this time
     Sends winds about the world ; hazels as well
     Are turning golden where the pale nuts swell ;
And one arm, one hand only, of a pear
     Has turned to scarlet, and a pinnacle
Of golden cypress glows in sunlight where
It lately glowed alone, the only gold thing there.

A young moon in a placid sky, pale gold,
   Is shining now, and peering as in wonder
Towards the world. What will it see when old ?
     What sombre powers of tyranny and plunder
     Hurled from their fortresses and trodden under
And all along the Côte d'Or lying prone ?
     While Liberty turns homeward through the thunder,
Home to the isles that she had so long known,
And home to Holland where she holds an ancient throne.

         September 23

And now a watcher of the woodlands sees
   How a young lime has decked herself to go
At Autumn's bidding to the dance of trees
     Where elm and oak will all their splendours show :
     Here a bright bracelet, there a little bow,
She seems to gather from a humble store,
     Which, every day, more full of gold will grow,
As though good fairies filled it, more and more
Coming across the fields by night with precious ore.

44

And now a whitebeam puts her brown dress on,
    Little by little, down over her head :
Her kith on hills of Kent through Summer shone
    Whenever a wind blew, and when it fled
    Their brilliance died and they were green instead
Of flashing white, beside the old dark yew,
    Which on a slope of downs where he was bred
Sees trees beside him of which only few
Are the old dwellers there that St. Augustine knew.

45

And blushingly a mountain-ash has joined
    The band of trees that wait for Autumn's dance.
These are the days when fairy gold is coined
    By every whim of the exuberance
    September knows, when pathways flash and glance
Under the beech-trees, and the splendour grows
    On earth and in the trees, where like a lance
Born by an elfin knight, whence no-one knows,
A golden ray of sun amongst bright branches glows.

46   *September 24*

And now a humble thorn puts on a dress
    As gorgeous as the stateliest that go
To Autumn's dance ; her kin about her press
    In wonder, having yet no more to show
    Than the bright beads that glitter row on row
Like little rubies : orange, pink and gold
    Her raiment is.   Like a green sea below
And foam above, a poplar's leaves are rolled,
For from the West a wind is blowing strong and cold.

47   *September 25*

An elder, which is looked on as a weed
    All through the Summer, beside tidy ways,
To whose wild flowers we give little heed,
    Whose night-like berries receive no-one's praise,
    Shows leaves that in these bright September days
Rival the rose.   Some swallows are still here
    Tracing their graceful curves across a haze
Of fine rain out of low clouds that appear
To rest upon the tops of beech-trees standing near.

48

And now the hazels shine with fairy gold
    Of the best carat ; paths are still more bright
Under the beech-trees, and the moss is old
    All through the woods, concealing from our sight
    Many a branch blown down some stormy night,
And making trunks of trees like curtained walls
    And covering all pathways, its green light
Dim-glowing down the corridors and halls
. That Nature makes in woods for her four festivals,

49

Where may be seen a people old and strange,
    That half-way between beasts and flowers seem :
All down the pathways of the woods they range
    And in the hollows of large trunks they teem,
    Mysterious folk, the people of a dream,
For so the toadstools look with their sly faces
    Hidden beneath huge hats as though a beam
Of moonlight might be deadly to those races
That haunt decaying stumps and revel in dank places.

50

And some over their white skins wear a brown
    Thick powder, and one wears a high grey hat,
And some are food for something, nibbled down,
    But not the deathcap, for none nibbles that ;
    And some are tall and lean, some round and fat.
And down one little path so many go
    That one would like to know what they were at,
But that is something that they will not show,
A secret of the woods which we shall never know.

51   *September 26*

Sometimes across a path and out of sight
    A small grey company upon some quest
Seems to go like red Indians through the light
    And shadows of the wood. An old stump dressed
    With moss, above which elder-trees have pressed
For some years, holds a brown crowd packed more dense
    Than any crowd of ours in streets compressed,
With its umbrellas up ; and an immense
Army of small dark folk lurk for the wood's defence.

52

Shadows are running through the fields for miles
    And, when they pass, an elm smiles suddenly
In glory, as a golden idol smiles
    For one whose faith in it leads him to see
    The sudden window in eternity
Opening on his idol, and the rays
    Illumining the lump of gold where he
Seeks for the meaning of the tide that sways
Man and the wandering stars far out beyond our ways.

53   *September 27*

Poplars to-day are flashing white as foam,
    For a North wind is riding through the sky.
Is it the one that to their other home
    Shall bear the swallows ? But the last ones fly
    Still by our windows here, although hard by
Their chariot waits and though they surely know
    The skies of Spain, unclouded, blue and high,
Expect them, or Aegean isles where slow
Liberty lame with so much wandering tries to go.

54   *September 28*

And now the golden season brings to view
    Chrysanthemums, gold tinted as with flame,
As though a touch of dawn were in their hue
    From sunrise in the land from which they came,
    And, with the glory with which woods proclaim
The ending of their splendour, these begin.
    And now that island of the land of fame,
Samothrace, sees her own guerillas win,
And winged Victory goes homeward to her kin.

55

Clear shines the mustard with its yellow glow,
    And now the partridge sees above its head
Withered potato-stalks, where chickweeds grow
    And heartsease still, although the clover's dead,
    Making a field look black with its dark head ;
And all the corn is cut, soon to be brought
    Home from the fields and stored in barn and shed.
And many see the sheaves without a thought
For those who saved our crops on far fields where they fought.

I looked once more from Tara, while the rain
    Loured from clouds all round us, and afar
Beyond the shadows of the darkened plain
    I saw fields gleaming, bright as emeralds are.
So may the future look beyond our war,
To those that gaze across the years to be.
    But I looked farther yet and saw a scar
Of tempest in the sky, as I can see
Far tumults that shall rise when Europe shall be free.

57

And then I saw like titans lying low,
    With limbs lopped off in battle, fallen beech.
These were the giants that a while ago
    Stood guarding an estate, which, as the breach
    In its old wall, and weedy pathways, teach,
Goes back to fields. At last, in every land,
    The weeds, the desert, or the jackals reach
To tower and garden. Here the bramble's hand
Grips in an instant at the South-west wind's command.

58 *September* 30

Suddenly sunset turns the beeches gold,
    As with a master-stroke, that Autumn's art
Cannot achieve until a wind more cold
    Shall blow to help it, though a little part
    Is done already and the beeches start
To dress as does the chestnut, and like bronze
    The sycamore appears, and willows dart
Silver and gold rays, and a creeper dons
Her scarlet dress and streams from walls like gonfalons.

59

Farewell September. In the deeps of Time,
    Where old months drift along a dateless shore,
Forgotten most, save where some chance-made rhyme
    Remembers them ; among those months of yore
    You need not fear oblivion : where the lore
Of freedom lingers you need only say
    I was September nineteen forty-four,
And all the ghosts of old months passed away
Will honour you, as we on earth for many a day.

OCTOBER

Now with a round moon looking on the mist
    October comes and, underneath a haze
That hides the future, dimly shows the gist
    Of vast events to our uncertain gaze,
    As shapes show vaguely under the moon's rays
And are not what they seem. All will be clear
    To students at their desks in distant days,
And dim confused disasters, to those near,
Far hence as orderly, neat problems will appear.

In marshes where the willowherb is over
    Grass of Parnassus lifts its dainty head ;
And here valerian outlives the clover
    And there a bunch of meadowsweet is shed
    All but one flower, and the bee is fed
No longer there. The news has come to-day
    That Kithera is free, where it is said
That Aphrodite rose out of the spray.
And surely Athens smiles, at last, by her blue bay.

A huge full moon came stealing through the trees,
    Loading the twigs with silver, overnight.
To-day out of the West a colder breeze
    Shadows the land with clouds, or brings to sight
    Towers and spires far off, in sudden light ;
And riding that cold breeze across gray sky
    Where the moon shone for them, a disc of white,
Went the last swallows, leaving bats to fly
In wavering circles where they lately darted by.

4

I mourn to-day for Warsaw's tragic fall.
  Poles brought me out of Greece three years ago
As Athens fell, and steered their ship through all
  The perils of those seas that used to know
  Scylla, and now an even deadlier foe
Was looking for our blood. They brought us past.
  And, surely not forgetting what we owe,
We have watched news of Warsaw, overcast
By such a thundercloud. And now it falls at last.

5 *October 4*

The wind that took the swallows on their way
  Has brought more gold to ornament the beech,
Like a strange traveller, whence none can say,
  With nuggets from the lands beyond men's reach
  Far to the North : some gift he brings for each,
And then to lands of asphodel or palm,
  Where the sun ripens orange, grape and peach,
He carries whom would go, singing his psalm
To troubled branches, till he finds the South and calm.

6

How vainly Hitler marched ! And with what glory
  Beethoven's powers served a better end,
And will outlive the Nazis' cruel story ;
  And long after a thousand years shall wend,
  Which Hitler claimed for his (but Heaven forfend),
Beethoven's voice shall ring, as through this night
  We hear his fifth concerto, which they send
Across the spaces where the swallows flight,
Music and wings alone, and passing in the height.

7 *October 5*

To-day in cloth-of-gold the beeches seem
  Sewn on green silk, and berberis-bushes flare
And clematis is bright and willows gleam
  And a dark ilex glooms and does not share
  The festive splendour that the trees prepare
All round it, and the end of leaves is near.
  And on a grander scale, amidst the glare
Of falling cities, Hitler's days appear
Drawing towards their end as swiftly as the year.

Autumn is full of ghosts of lakes long dead
    Which haunt the evening, when the tits fly home
And twitter on their twigs, while overhead
    The rooks go cawing through the lucid dome
    Of the pale sky, and bats come out to roam
And ducks are on the wing, and the grey ghost
    Of an old lake creeps back over the loam
Where once it dwelt. At last we hear the host
Of Hitler slips away from the Morean coast.

9 October 6

All night the ghostly lake hung in the air,
    And dawn stole up and dressed the ghost in gold ;
And now one would not know it had been there,
    Had not the spider caught it in a fold
    Of his fine web, and morning sees him hold
The shrunken ghost that lately hid the trees
    And softly over all our pastures rolled,
And on large leaves and blades of grass one sees
Drops that a while ago were the ghost's panoplies.

10

Again the ghostly lake appears at dusk.
    Autumn has power to call up such things,
And gild the leaves and split the chestnut's husk,
    And send the bats upon their wanderings
    To hunt for flies where lately swallows' wings
Flashed in the same pursuit. Heavy and deep
    The mist lies over the green fields, and flings
Its arms round little mounds, and seems to creep
Stealthily in the still where the dark trees rise steep.

11 October 7

Acorns and chestnuts lie upon the ground,
    And beechnuts, which will lure the pigeons here
Out of far lands, and walnuts may be found
    In split green husks. In marshes still appear
    Sheep-scabious, and though meadowsweet is sere
A few blooms linger, and the watercress
    Is all in flower ; there the swift snipe steer
Crazily through the air, and hares from stress
Of life on guarded lands find shelter in distress.

12

Borodin's piece of music, In The Steppes
    Of Central Asia, came to us to-day
Across the ether : like bees caught in skeps
        The music hums in wireless sets ; the bray
        Of horns is brought to us from far away,
The slow procession moving to the West,
        The camels and the Tartars ; then the grey
Horizon hides them to the last plumed crest
And the last horn is heard and all the wild notes rest.

13 October 8

Still Japanese anemones survive
    The loss of Summer, and mauve daisies hold
The garden now, where dahlias still alive
        Flaunt their late glory, and the rose grows old.
        Now nuts out of their canopy of gold
Fall from the hazels, and when men are all
        Gone from the garden, sometimes in the cold
And hush of evening down the garden wall
The squirrel comes for stores, to have when snows shall fall.

14

Now ash-trees turn a pale gold one by one,
    Looking, against the dark gold of the beech,
Like fairy gold, not minted from the sun,
        But rather from the moon's rays, when the screech
        Of the white owl warns mortals out of reach
Of magic, and the mystery of the glen
        Where dwell the folk against whom good men preach,
The folk who at the back of nine in ten
Of Irish minds hold thrones not yet usurped by men.

15

And winter-jasmine blooms upon a wall.
    And now three primroses have shown their faces
Under a sheltered bank where chestnuts fall
        And where the winds that dance in open spaces
        Will not disturb them till the snow's last traces,
When all around them they will see their kin
        Welcome back April to the mossy places.
But to gaze hence to half our planet's spin
Is far indeed to look, with the war yet to win.

16

Once to look on to Spring from golden leaves
   Were but to turn one page of history,
But now to look from this year's harvest's sheaves
   To banks of primroses were suddenly
   To turn through many volumes that shall be
Written about our story, all to tell
   Whether mankind is to know liberty
Or whether all through Europe men shall dwell
As slaves within the wire encircling Hitler's hell.

17 October 9

Almost as though Earth borrowed from the dawn
   Some fragments of the splendour of the sky
A berberis is leaning on a lawn,
   Shining with leaves and berries, while near by
   A chestnut with this glory seems to vie,
Gorgeous in pink and orange, and the blue
   Of grapes is now its loveliest, where high
The bunches hang, or with a golden hue
The muscats' bunches gleam like sunlight shining through.

18 October 10

But better my glass houses now in Kent
   Than any here : there the grey glass is lying
Along the earth, where long since it was sent
   On stormy nights when Goering's men were flying,
   Whose wild wings all my garden was defying,
So that it has its share in all things free,
   Having shared ruin when the world seemed dying,
And in the calmer days that are to be
Its fruits shall see some light that these fruits will not see.

19

Some music of Sibelius blew to-day
   Over the ether, calling up wild plains
And forests dark with firs, and far away
   Sometimes a lonely horn whose haunting strains
   Blow over ice through desolate domains
Enchanted by this Finnish symphony.
   Of all our works what monument remains,
Preserving ought in human memory,
Longer than music can with its strange wizardry ?

More and more gorgeously the beeches all
    Array themselves with gay vicissitude,
But the great oaks stand resolute and tall,
    Still unaffected by the passing mood
    That has come down upon the gleaming wood,
Not changing yet their fashion, though the wold
    Flashes as though the limes and ashes stood
Draped in exuberance of cloth of gold,
On which the oaks glance down, unchangeable and old.

Like palaces of gold the chestnuts stand,
    Or many heavens for as many creeds,
Built not far hence, but upon solid land ;
    And every day is seen, by him who heeds,
    A new adornment upon shrubs and weeds,
As though some traffic were between lands known
    And legendary vales in faery meads
Where an elf-king upon a magic throne
Makes golden leaves with runes written by him alone.

Even a rainy day can scarce obscure
    The beauty of the Autumn, and the grey
Of a low cloud rises above the lure
    Of golden boughs, as some grey satin may
    Enclose a brooch or bracelet. Far away
Pigeons have heard that beech-nuts may be found
    Upon our paths, and flocks begin to stray
Into our woods, slanting in circles round,
Then settling in the trees or gathering on the ground.

23

Birds, butterflies and seeds of many flowers
    On daily winds blew by us in times past,
But something more comes on the passing hours
    To all of us in these days ; from the vast
    Of ether comes what never rode the blast
Of winds a while ago, and music's bars
    Over the world to all of us are cast,
Roaming between the hill-tops and the stars,
The greatest wonder Man contrived between two wars.

24

To-day Ravel's Bolero came, that strange
    And haunting outburst of fierce energy,
Such energy as, given other range,
      Might have wrecked cities, or new policy
      Enforced in place of old ; and we might be,
In spite of both, much where we were before ;
    But he who fashions a new melody
Brings Mother Earth new treasure for her store,
And she has something gained that she had not of yore.

25

Athens is free, with all her rose-clad bowers,
    Her friendly pine-woods, and the streets I know,
Slanting up Lycabettus to the flowers !
      All, all are free after these years of woe.
      The little gardens where the almonds grow
Are free at last, and the immortal stone
    On the Acropolis, whose golden glow
Smiles on our day from days we have not known
And sees at last, at last, the enemy o'erthrown.

26   *October* 14

Her bells from every church are ringing now,
    As I have heard them ring for victory.
One I remember swinging from a bough
      Beside a small church. Now exultantly
      It rings again, to tell that men are free
In Athens. But who live of friends I knew ?
    Who from the dark of that calamity
That lay three years on Athens has come through
Past such brutalities, famine and slaughter ? Who ?

27

Again Sibelius on the air to-day.
    It is as though in any Southern land
Heaven was infinite and far away,
      While in the North its outer ramparts stand
      So close upon the hill-tops, or the strand
Of a bleak sea, that to its cloudy girth
    A singer need no more than stretch a hand
To pluck a melody and bring to earth
Some air that he has heard amidst the angels' mirth.

28

And still I dream of Greece ; that tawdry banner
    That for three years flapped from the Parthenon,
Flouting Athene in this flagrant manner,
    That wretched emblem, must by now be gone,
    The gaudy folds of its vermilion
Lying with loot and scraps of food and tins
    In baggage of an army, hurried on
By dreams of cheating vengeance for its sins,
While Liberty pursues and her forlorn hope wins.

29

October 15

A while ago only the bees were free
    Along Hymettus. Lately only they
Between the mountain and the sapphire sea
    Had leave to live their lives and go their way
    Unhindered by the rules of those that say
Heil Hitler, and they only did not know
    The well-planned famine by which Germans slay.
Now like a bitter sea those Germans go,
Which over fields and farms of pleasant lands did flow.

30

They will go Northward, leaving Marathon
    Upon their right, through Thebes, and past the shore
Of what was Lake Copaïs ; Helicon
    Will watch their flight, and the mount famed of yore,
    Parnassus, and the hills the Vlachs explore
In Winter ; and, if they so far should fare,
    Olympus will frown down upon them, hoar
With watching human history, aware
That Liberty for long was never vanquished there.

31

But where are the brave women that we knew
    In Athens when the thunderbolt was falling ?
The men, I know, are fighting ; but the true
    Brave-hearted women facing those appalling
    Three years and more, when tyranny was brawling
Triumphantly through Europe, where are they ?
    For they were no Lavals or Quislings crawling
Before successful rapine to obey.
What has become of them ? How many live to-day ?

Two whitebeams stand like pillars of gold gates,
    And all beyond them shines, even when air
And sky are grey ; a golden yew abates
    Its splendour in these days when everywhere
    Trees it outshone a while ago are fair
With so much gold.   The flowers scarce know how
    To hold erect under the weight they bear,
And the chrysanthemums seem lonely now
While from the garden goes a glory to the bough.

Again a rainy day, but sunlight seems
    Stored in the leaves that flash with summer's light.
The rain's grey ghosts drift by where an elm gleams
    As fair as sunset glorying, before night,
    While glows and shines this foliage in despite
Of winter, which the chestnuts know is near
    And now show all their splendour in our sight,
And through the beeches too has gone a fear
As winter's far-off step is heard, as these things hear.

Strange that a rumour to the countryside
    To tell that any town was paved with gold
Should ever have blown hither.   While there glide
    These leaves along the air and strew the mould
    It is a wonder that no tale is told
To men of the grey streets that gold is here,
    To lure them from their noisy ways to old
And quiet ways, where all our paths appear
A mass of fairy gold, fresh-minted every year.

35

We hear the Averof, her exile done,
    Lies under Athens, whence she sailed away
On the nineteenth of April, forty-one,
    With the Carlisle ; and where they stood at bay,
    With other giants, crept a little stray
Polovtsian cargo-boat through sleepy seas
    Dreaming of sapphires, when their only spray
Was made by bombs ; and so she came to peace,
Guarded by these good ships.   May their fame never cease.

Even to towns, however grey and sober
    Their ways may be, some gleam of Autumn goes.
Even in towns the splendour of October
    Flashes down streets, and out of gardens glows
    After the sun has faded like the rose.
And sometimes at a street's end I can see
    Dim mountains, and who looks upon them knows
That, harsh and hurried though a city be,
He has not yet lost all touch with eternity.

As though they both were exiles and so came
    Into a city, birds and men meet there.
Man, the wild hunter, in the towns is tame,
    As mallards know and pigeons, when they dare
    To walk beside him in a city's square,
Wanderers all of them and far from home,
    Far from the lucid spaces of the air,
Far from the dim woods or the bright sea's foam
And far indeed from peace, these fellow-wanderers roam.

So early from the Arctic or the shore
    Of Scotland or the outer Hebrides
The geese have come : one old grey-lag before
    The others flies alone, as though he sees
    Some rigour of the winter that will freeze
The lakes before their time : the others fly
    An hour behind him ; it may be that they
Seeing their leader rise, had wondered why
He left so soon, and then followed reluctantly.

39

And from the North Sibelius came again,
    For his fifth symphony was played to-day.
Narrow indeed would be a man's demesne
    If nothing from the North or South should stray
    Ever into the fields where he may stay.
The geese bring rumours of some lands afar,
    And something more than what their voices say
Sibelius tells, guiding our dreams where are
Forests that dance with storms beneath the Northern star.

40

The pigeons that were here a while ago
    Have told the others that the nuts are good
Under the beech-trees, all well-filled, and so
    A cloud of them has come upon the wood,
    Lured from a long way off to find the food
That this year offers, for not every year
    Gives them so much, as though Dame Nature's mood
Were one year to feed pigeons, but would veer
Like a wild wind and soon some other call would hear.

41   *October 22*

There is a splendour in the cherries now
    That can almost outshine the chestnut's glory,
And every leaf is flaming on the bough.
    Like a huge giant in a fairy story
    A clematis has stretched its predatory
Long arms through a small garden, where it grows
    Wreathed with its mass of flowers grey and hoary ;
And sometimes through its folds an apple glows,
While in the weeds below is fading the last rose.

42

A beech is shining against blue-grey sky
    Golden as any sunset, still aglow
When all is dim and bats begin to fly.
    And now we hear how Russian armies flow
    Into a forest where a while ago
The Germans used to hunt : in many a den
    And leafy covert lurking beasts must know
The danger changes, and through every glen
Down which they ever fled, men are now hunting men.

43   *October 23*

And now the Spanish chestnuts turn to gold
    And showers sweep with winds across the view,
Turning the beeches' glow a little cold,
    To flash again in all its glorious hue
    As the cloud races eastward from the blue.
All shades of gold are shining in bright air
    Which flocks of wood-pigeons are streaming through
To find the treasure that has brought them there
By ways no man has sung, whereof we are unaware.

44

Two years ago, as when stilled waters stand
    One moment in their world-wide outward sweep,
Then tremble and swing back to the far land
    Out of the hush and mystery of the deep,
    So at El Alamein after that neap
That had swept Liberty so far away
    The tide of war stirred in the desert's sleep
And has flowed shorewards ever since that day
Till under its huge weight the German cities sway.

45 *October 24*

A North wind blows and has cleared all the sky
    And brought green plover out of distant spaces.
Over our fields in little flocks they fly,
    And wheel and wander over marshy places.
    Southward the woodcock will soon set their faces.
Far hills shine faint, as though dissolved in steam
    Were silver ingots, or in heaven traces
Of uncreated hills were just agleam,
Or as one might see heights of elfland in a dream.

46

Geese and green plover. It may be the Norns,
    Dark among crags of Norway, mean to send
An early winter. Berries on the thorns
    Are hanging ready. Do these birds portend
    A bitter winter? But till Hitler's end
It will be bitter without help of wrath
    From any wind that makes the oak-trees bend,
Or all the storms December can send forth,
Or any hail or snow that ever left the North.

47 *October 25*

With drooping leaves of apricot and pink
    On stems of crimson now the dogwood glows.
As in a ballroom candles flare and sink,
    And light is in the East and slowly grows
    Till it is dawn, and still no dancer knows ;
So from a chestnut few leaves float away
    And from a pear-tree its bright foliage goes,
But Autumn's festival is still as gay,
And golden branches like bejewelled dancers sway.

48 　　　　　　　　　　 *October 26*

Some barley sheaves, where a tilled field runs near
　　To marshes, stand like legendary things
Which rarely in the human fields appear,
　　An elvish company whose wanderings
　　Have brought them from the wilder lands where clings
A white mist to the grasses. Shapes like these
　　Seen in the grey Autumnal evenings
And told of round the fire by folk at ease
Add to the awe of night still darker mysteries.

49

No trailing shape of rain the wind may blow,
　　No shadow on the earth or in the sky,
Can spoil the splendour of the beeches' glow
　　Or dim the cherries as it passes by.
　　There are no grey days where such trees are nigh.
No landscape appears dull, or even sober,
　　Lit by these chestnuts which with sunset vie,
When robed by Autumn, that enchanted rober,
Glowing with all the gold and glory of October.

50 　　　　　　　　　　 *October 27*

Bare twigs are showing on the tops of trees
　　And all the pathways shine with fallen gold,
For last night from the West a colder breeze
　　Came to the beeches. From the Northern cold
　　The jack-snipe are arriving where grows old
The lesser spearwort, and that flower Apollo
　　Knew on his mountain falls into the mould,
And rushes grow ; and to that marshy hollow
The snipe of Northern lands over the sea will follow.

51 　　　　　　　　　　 *October 28*

If cloth-of-gold grew threadbare ere kings fell,
　　Or jewels from their crowns dropped one by one,
If paint on gilded gates should flake and swell
　　And banners dropped before their reigns were done,
　　Like Autumn's story would their story run ;
But they fall suddenly, while Autumn's story
　　Is of leaves drifting downward in the sun,
The gradual disappearing of a glory
Even more brief than Man's, than his more transitory.

75

Yet still like ragged gold the chestnuts gleam
   And still the beeches, while the twilight fades,
Until the moon is master of the scheme
   And no more colour glitters in the glades
   Or in the sky but his, and with the shades
Of night the bright trees dress themselves, as though
   They stole away disguised, kings and their aides,
Leaving the splendour of some gorgeous show
From which the time had come for them and theirs to go.

         October 29

To-day in a clear sky the sun has set
   Beyond the beeches in their tattered gold,
And through the silence one can feel a threat,
   As though already from some arctic wold
   Winter approached us. A moon twelve days old
Steals through the trees to pry about the world.
   And what a world to look on for that cold
Far watcher, with so many smoke-clouds curled
Over so many hearths, and all to ruin hurled ;

Save only where we sleep and dream of peace
   In Ireland, but our dream is all untrue.
We are not neutral. Its own silly fleece
   Guards from the hungry wolf no straying ewe.
   Other men fight for us ; to them is due
Our thankfulness at harvest-time. How near
   We came to waking, to see truth shine through
And turn our dream to nightmare, though seen clear
By daylight. We are saved. But Hell was nearly here.

         October 30

The West side of the beeches is blown bare
   By a cold wind, but bright among them strays
The sunlight, bringing back their former air
   Of splendour, as may memory to ways
   Whence grandeur has passed on with other days.
To-day the Hungarian march through ether came.
   If men's blood thrilled not when such music plays
There would be hope Bellona might grow tame
And parliaments stop war as one stamps out a flame.

56

Now from the dogwood golden leaves are streaming
  Where stand their red stems by the beeches old,
As though a dynasty, awaked from dreaming
  One night by revolution, should behold
  Its guards stripped of their ornaments of gold
Until their crimson was all bare.   And now
  Another light comes riding through the cold,
Brighter than any on the beech's bough,
Like a usurper with new gold upon his brow.

57

So comes the moon, and a gay retinue
  Of ghosts of streams comes with it, plumed and curled.
A few bats flutter, darker than the blue
  Of the dark sky, and magic holds the world,
  Or some strange power along moonbeams hurled
We know not in the day, something that goes
  Leaving no track upon the grass dew-pearled,
Guarding its secret even from the rose,
Unknown, unless some gnarled and haunted willow knows.

58   *October* 31

A young elm all in gold stands as though she
  Waited to dance, while all around were old
Or weary or reduced to poverty,
  With wide rents showing in their cloth-of-gold,
  Except the oaks, which still seem to withhold
Their notice from the chestnut's sudden glory
  And all the splendid garments which enfold
The beeches, but stand reverend and hoary,
Looking with little heed on the elm's briefer story.

59

To-night a full moon shines on Hallow Eve,
  When ghosts are loose along the little lanes
From every graveyard, as the folk believe
  Where any of the old lore yet remains.
  Behind the glow of cottage windowpanes
There are strange customs, hidden from my sight
  As haply they were hidden from the Danes,
And practised even yet upon this night,
While the ghosts watch outside till the first streak of light.

And so October ends. Has it done all
    We hoped of it ? At least it has freed Greece
And that is a superb memorial
    For any month, although the wings of Peace
    Are not yet visible and no decrease
Comes in the raging torrent of men's blood
    And though the flames of cities do not cease.
For Greek soil is where Liberty first stood ;
And how should she survive, with Greece in servitude ?

NOVEMBER

November 1

The fields to-day with a grey mist are fraught,
 As though not all the ghosts went home last night
To neighbouring graveyards ; some the spider caught
 In his slung hammocks, where they glimmer white,
 And some are trailing hence with the gold light
That drives them home. A birch stands lightly draped
 With golden gauze that does not hide from sight
Her lithe white limbs, as delicately shaped
As those of fay or faun from elfin land escaped.

2 *November* 2

Again a mist to-day, but nothing dims
 The glory of the chestnuts, even though
Their robes be threadbare, showing their great limbs.
 Like mountain-tops of gold far elm-trees show.
 And golden is the larch. On lawns below
The beeches, costly robes a dryad wore
 Seem to be lying, though with dimmer glow
Than that with which they shone a while before
When they and sunlight seemed to blend in one clear ore.

3 *November* 3

A sunset flames, but all the shining West
 Is scarce more splendid than the gold that gleams
Eastward upon a Spanish chestnut's crest,
 Which like some precipice's summit gleams,
 Fashioned of pure gold in a land of dreams ;
And beeches, though disrobing, still possess
 Some gems to twinkle in the level beams,
And there is still a splendour in their dress
With which to face the sun, though it grows less and less.

79

F

4   *November* 4

A wind has risen up like a new law
    To tell the beeches that the time is gone
For those bright robes that the woods lately saw,
      And there are bare limbs now where splendours shone
      And leaves are lying lost on earth ; anon
They rise up giddily, to dance before
    The whirlwind in a last bright cotillon,
For a few flashing moments to restore
The splendour that they knew, then sink, and rise no more.

5   *November* 5

Far from the beeches on a level lawn
    A sheet of leaves is lying like the dress
Of some bright spirit that had danced till dawn
      With the West wind, until in weariness
      The wind had fallen, still in his caress
That gleaming robe ; but the bright spirit far
    Is gone upon her way with streaming tress
Beyond the hills to whisper to a star
(Forgetting that brief dance) where mighty spirits are.

6   *November* 6

Gravely and slowly now the oaks put on
    Their cloth-of-gold, and many trees are bare.
Last night I saw, when the last hill had shone,
      A white haze rising under uplands where
      A sleeping silent city had its lair.
Its golden lights came out under the haze,
    Then came the dark hills and the lucid air.
And, as earth darkened, the aërial ways
Grew brighter, or so seemed to my enraptured gaze.

7   *November* 7

A West wind darkens heaven ; earth is cold.
    Oak, lime and elm, and sometimes sycamore,
Hoard still some fragment of their flying gold,
      And gold is all the larch, but the great store
      Of Autumn's wealth is wasted, as with war
The nations' wealth. Winter will soon be here.
    I saw his scouts, which a short way before
Ride the cold air and tell us he is near ;
And all the hints that warn of snow and ice are here.

8

One told me how he saw, two months since, stand
    A stork beside a bog, a refugee.
How did it know there was a lazy land
    That neither helped nor hated Liberty,
    Where there would be no furious energy
Spent on a cause concerning only Man ?
    Where doubtless it applauds our apathy
And finds perhaps some value in our plan,
As such a bird might do, although I never can.

9 *November* 8

Michaelmas daisies in the garden now
    Watch the sad end of all the other flowers
Except chrysanthemums, but bough by bough
    A splendour as of sunset on cloud-towers
    Touches the leaves of raspberries, though showers
Of bright leaves strew the paths ; and vines grow red
    And currant bushes have made gleaming bowers,
And just outside, above a potting-shed,
A larch with one bright flash lifts up its golden head.

10 *November* 9

Now in the sky clear notes are often heard,
    As though a spirit with a flute of gold
Wandered at will ; too magic for a bird
    Such music seems, and like some story told
    Of strange enchantments in the days of old.
Yet look, and you will see the golden plover
    Sailing in high bright air, till from the cold
They drop to fields that mist begins to cover
When windows start to glow, and lover walks with lover.

11

Then up and down a field a flock will fly,
    Like a huge angel whose wings brush the ground
And whistle with a curious melody,
    Heard by some shepherd when all other sound
    Is sleeping ; long they dance in their swift round
Upon the lower levels of the air,
    And not till night is silent and profound
Do they come down from their dim ways to share
The solid sheltering earth with goat and sheep and hare.

The darker shapes of the green plover too
    Pass up and down, but on a lazy wing,
Strange company for those that travel through
    The airy spaces, whose swift travelling
    Is almost like an arrow's ; yet they cling
To the same fields, and are the farmer's friends,
    Hunting the wire-worm that lies burrowing
Under the wheat and grass at the roots' ends
And, working in the dark, a meagre harvest sends.

Now comes the day on which I hoped in vain
    The war would end. How often on this date
Throve the vain hopes which said that war again
    Would not break out in our time, and that Fate
    Would heed the argument of our debate
And with changed heart would rule by other ways
    Than her old way, letting the vote have weight
That sword and cannon had in other days,
And rosy outlooks loomed on our besotted gaze.

Now stand the beeches like defeated kings
    In exile, clad in tatters of their ermine
Torn by disaster and long wanderings
    Far from their palaces, where now the vermin
    Run through great curtains and the wood has worm in.
For we should scarcely wonder if the plan
    Our history makes and parliaments determine
Were but like Nature's way, which her child, Man,
Would oft forsake for his grand schemes, but seldom can.

A grey day closes in with haze and rain,
    But in the narrow circle of the view
The oak-trees shine, and elms, and what remain
    Of glories that the beech-trees lately knew,
    And larches and a golden lime or two ;
And earth has her own beauty now, a lawn
    Shining with fallen leaves the West wind blew
Down from the beeches ; like a gleam of dawn
It glimmers in the grey till light is quite withdrawn.

16

Sunset ; and pigeons in their thousands go
    In curves and circles over the high trees.
Lower their circles swing until as low
    As branches are, then in, against the breeze,
    They fly, and sleep, and though the night may freeze
They keep warm by an art that we have lost,
    Replaced by all the things that give us ease,
And shelter us and clothe us, at the cost
Of failing by ourselves to face a night of frost.

17

And then like an enormous dragon's wing,
    Somewhere between a whisper and a sigh,
Or like a waterfall's far murmuring,
    A multitude of starlings hurries by
    Along their pathway in the pale blue sky
Going to their far home. And, last of those
    That wander and that through the evening fly,
The duck come dark, as the last daylight goes,
And drop with rush of wings where the dim water glows.

18   *November* 13

So strong seems Nature here, so weak man's hands,
    That all he builds, whether in mud or stone,
Seems to yield sooner than in other lands
    To moss and ivy from the South-west blown.
    I saw a cottage time had overthrown,
And round it like victorious ogres stood
    Old apple-trees, which men had claimed to own,
But which now came with all their mossy brood
Into the roofless rooms with clawing limbs of wood.

19

From Arctic night to where the sea-weeds sway
    Goes down the deadly Tirpitz. Good men flew
And good stars guided them to where she lay,
    And no more harm remains for her to do.
    Who went to sea in these years never knew
When he would meet her. Perils of the sea
    Are fewer by one peril, and the blue
Is free of this great monster, as soon free
From Hitler's cruelty the land, at last, will be.

The glory of the beeches is all gone
　　Save where a few preserve some tattered piece
Of a lost grandeur, such as might have shone
　　On one hand of an exile, one thin crease
　　Of a great robe, when robes and jewels cease
To be that wanderer's lot, but treasured still
　　For old days' sake and memory's caprice.
So stand these beeches all along the hill
Clutching small sad remains, as fallen grandeur will.

And chestnuts, yet more splendid in their day,
　　Are all bare now, although their Spanish kin
Still to the dawn and setting sun display
　　Their glowing southern raiments, that begin
　　To show rents, gaping as the gold gets thin.
And bare is every limb of every ash.
　　Yet in a wood when sunrays wander in,
Sometimes a young birch gives a golden flash
With its last finery, which winds already lash.

Last night a frost came brightening the land,
　　And now the fields are green and shadows white,
For only where a tree or buildings stand
　　Between it and the sun the frost is bright
　　By what we call noon.　In the fading light
Yesterday, as small birds went home to trees,
　　I saw the dark shape of a woodcock flight.
Perhaps already from across the seas
These wanderers reach our woods, riding some bitter breeze.

23

A storm is roaring in the air to-night,
　　And in the ether is the rage of man,
For on the wireless we can hear the fight
　　In Holland, the machine-guns in the van
　　And further back the guns, whose salvos span
The field of battle, so Man's anger towers
　　Up from the earth, and with the thunder can
Move round the world among the winds and showers,
Hobnobbing in the heights with elemental powers.

Yesterday's frost and last night's wind together
    Have taken the last leaves, except the cloak
Of cloth-of-gold which in this wintry weather
        Is clutched about his old limbs by the oak ;
        And rain into the soil begins to soak,
Till ditches run with streams ; and far hills show,
        As though out of a dream they lately woke
To smile a little on the world below,
Foretelling further rain, and when it comes they go.

Beechnuts and acorns still provide the food
    Of clouds of pigeons, which across grey sky
Pass with a roar of wings from wood to wood,
        That now have laid their robes of splendour by,
        Save where the oak preserves a memory
Of his old grandeur, or the storm has missed
        An elm's last leaves, which give a lonely sigh,
Like little creatures that an alchemist
Had turned to sudden gold before their last breath hissed.

26

And while I watch the last of Autumn's glory,
    Or see in memory the Summer's flowers,
Or look at the calm hills and ruins, hoary
        With ivy that so grandly robes their towers,
        Or fields forever verdant with mild showers,
All, all at peace, I think of those that fought
        To keep for us these bright untroubled hours
Who, but for them, had been, like Belgians, brought
To look in Havoc's face, which cares for speeches naught.

27

And some were young friends near, who had no care
    For the mock shelter of neutrality ;
Malachy Simonds, lost in the night air
        Of unknown spaces of a foreign sky,
        He and his bomber missing since July,
And Herbert Radcliffe, never heard of more
        Since Arnhem, and de Stacpoole where winds sigh
Along grey seas the Navy watches o'er,
Keeping disaster from our else-unguarded shore.

28

And two young Bomfords lost too. Let these names,
  And Ian Blacker's, live to a far day.
Let all who see their thatch untouched by flames
  Honour the men that kept those flames away.
  For these I name, and more than I can say,
Held back the flames, but not neutrality :
  Denmark was neutral too, and Norroway
And . . ., but of what use can the long list be ?
Let any see the facts who may have eyes to see.

29

November 19

The garden now, in mourning for the rose,
  Is dark and desolate ; the old grey dress
The hazels wore under their mantles, shows
  Now that the gold is gone ; a wilderness
  Of dead stalks bend to earth under the stress
Of rain and wind and winter ; on a bough
  Bare of its leaves, shining in loneliness,
An apple lingers, and through branches sough
The winds that bring the rain, and all is sodden now.

30

The floods return, as though an old bog planned
  To hold the ground that it has held before.
Old names are used now up and down the land,
  And it may be that with these words of yore
  Old ways may come again and time restore
The bog where pasture is, and we shall see
  Our politics rejecting more and more
The progress of the rest, until we be
Back as when raths were built and Firbolgs still were free.

31

Fewer and fewer as the Year grows old
  Are his dependants in their splendour seen,
And none he dresses now in cloth-of-gold
  Except the oaks and larch ; and the dark green
  Of spruce and fir shows vividly between
The bare limbs of the beech, as might appear
  Some faun's or dryad's child, of lineage mean,
But yet immortal, by a hero's bier,
Knowing that he himself need never go from here.

Higher the floods are rising, a wind mourns
    Out of the West, and rumour comes to say
The geese are in, flown from their distant bourns
    To bogs near by ; all signs that on the way
    Is Winter. Sometimes, lonely and astray,
Is seen a flower on the garden wall,
    But it is desolate amid decay :
Gone are its brilliant comrades hence, and all
The blooms of Summer and the fruits of Autumn fall.

33

As in a land lost to an old regime
    Some lone survivor of a fallen line
Might from young fancy or an old man's dream,
    Or for the sake of what's called auld lang syne,
    Wear once again a cloak of grand design
And stand awhile remembering past days
    And courts before a dynasty's decline ;
So stand a few oaks in the level rays
Still gold, while sinks the sun into a wintry haze.

34

And now a young moon through the evening sails.
    If any spirit looked at us from there,
Knowing so much of peace in lunar vales
    How it would gaze at our wild scenes, how stare
    At all those cities lying layer on layer,
Haply preferring our fierce energy
    To the calm spaces void of, even, air,
Haply preferring calm, nor he nor we
Finding the perfect mean 'twixt war and lunar sea.

Now tributaries hurry to the Boyne,
    Full to their edges, and Boyne sweeps along
Wide with the floods that from all valleys join
    His waters, and he goes by proud and strong.
    The leaves have left the hedges, but a throng
Of berries flashes redly in the sun.
    Ice moves the snipe from bogs, but not for long
And before noon they drop back one by one
To unfrequented lands, where a few hares may run.

Now to their houses the chrysanthemums
    Retire from rain and cold ; if they were men
They would light pipes by fires, while the wind hums
    Outside, and sit and think of those days when
    The rose was with them, draw the blinds and then
Forget the winter.   There their splendours shine
    Golden as kingcups, bright brown as the wren,
Pink as the rose, dark crimson as the wine
They make from bluest grapes in some far-southern vine.

37

Now a few oaks, still glowing in the grey
    Between the sunset and the fall of night,
Watch wider floods ; the starlings on their way
    To roost far off, pass over on their flight
    And bats go wavering round, and it is night.
The sky is grey and starless, with no moon ;
    The shapes of trees stand dark and floods show white.
Over them rises an old Danish doon ;
Only its outline, black with branches, will show soon.

38   *November 23*

The clouds have gathered round and no hills show.
    In any high green field now snipe appear,
Driven by flood out of the bogs below.
    A heron watches by a rushing weir,
    Knowing the water and the time of year,
And more of fish than we shall ever learn,
    A still shape standing with a deadly spear.
A moon half full veils and unveils in turn
A golden face with clouds which warm winds drive and spurn.

39

Strasburg at last !   The French are back again !
    Often I saw her statue crowned with towers
Seated in Paris, when Alsace-Lorraine
    Was still lost, solemn wreaths of funeral flowers
    Laid at her feet ; and like immortal powers
Her sister cities seemed to mourn her state.
    I saw her later in the happy hours
When she was free, then heard of her dread fate.
Now Liberty and she are weeping in her gate ;

Weeping but happy, thinking of the years
    When they were lost and all the world was sad,
And some had soaring hopes and, some, dark fears
    That both were lost for ever, yet how glad
    Are Liberty and Strasburg, Strasburg clad
With her own flags again, and Liberty
    Honoured once more, where lately all men had
Stretched out an arm and cried a foolish cry
In honour of a creed of world-wide slavery.

41

Seagulls that know these floods and when they rise
    Have found them now, and bright against the grey
Their white shapes show. And now through gleaming skies
    Cloud-mountains golden at the end of day
    Seem to foretell a new wind on its way,
A stranger coming from a distant strand
    Over their shining passes, that display
The gem-like spaces of an empty land
Ruled over by the moon, which looks to the left hand.

42

The stranger was the North wind, which has blown
    Cloudland with every peak out of the sky,
Leaving the vault like a vast precious stone,
    Through which at times the golden plover fly
    And sometimes curlews, whence they can descry
What harder weather the North wind will bring.
    Now, broader yet, the Boyne goes rolling by
Filling his valleys. Half an orange ring
At sunset made the West like some enchanted thing.

43

A flock of pigeons to a beech-tree flies
    And feeds below it, for though now is gone
The glory of the trees, their treasure lies
    Thick underneath those boughs on which there shone
    Lately the golden leaves, vermilion
At sunset : like grey poultry feeding there
    The pigeons crowd, then fly in hundreds on,
And busy with their traffic seems the air,
So new to us, to them so old a thoroughfare.

White fields beneath a red dawn show the weather
  The stranger brought over the peaks of gold
Out of the North. The floods and sky together
  Shone in the morning. Now the winter's cold
  Moves woodcock into woods, where trunks grown old
And mossy stand between them and the might
  Of winds that sweep across the open wold,
As men find shelter by the warmth and light
Of firesides, when cold mist brings on the Winter's night.

45

To-day from ether came the Siegfried idyll,
  Wagner's strong music that inflames the blood
Of Germans. But we shall not solve the riddle
  By stopping Wagner, even if we could,
  Or stopping armaments, for nations would
Fight just as well with knives, nor shall we find
  Some means of government to tame the brood
Of nations, something none has yet divined,
And make non-combatant the whole of humankind.

46

Haply I had more readers if I wrote
  I foresaw peace for ever, but a lie
Had best have not one reader. What I note
  In the thick mists of Time, and what my eye
  Can see around me in the earth and sky,
I write for any that may care to read,
  Caring to turn a glance on days gone by.
And here is truth, however plain my screed.
I have no need for less. And is there any need ?

47

The Irish wind, the South-west wind, has blown
  The frost away, and over floods there ride
Small clouds sun-tinted. Now the oak alone
  Has any tattered remnant of the pride
  Of Autumn : even that is streaming wide
On winds now, with the pigeons ; and the gold
  Has left the earth, save where at eventide
A flood has caught the glorious and cold
Light of the setting sun's last blessing to the wold.

48

Then even that gold fades, and gold more magic
        Steals through the wood, as the moon comes to peer
Upon a world that never was more tragic
        Than what it now is. But why write it here ?
        Readers far hence will see the story clear,
Which is confused for us by smoking rubble
        With glories flashing through it : we, too near,
See all our era like a breaking bubble,
And fire advancing yet, where our race stands like stubble.

49   *November* 29

Under the moon wild voices may be heard
        Of ducks upon the floods, as though the night
Were given speech by them, which had no word
        Without these voices. Now the lunar light
        Leads snipe from marshes on their long strange flight
To bogs where all the heath is withering,
        And red grass grows by mosses green and bright,
And tracks of hares or men go wandering
A little way ; and cease in wastes of moss and ling.

50

And into them there falls and dies the heather
        Year after year, and the slow centuries
Bind the old bloom and stalks and moss together
        To make the brown soil out of which arise
        Gardens where no-one goes, where the hare lies
And where at the full moon from far around
        The snipe will make his pilgrimage, and flies
Back to the green and less enchanted ground
When the moon rises late and is no longer round.

51

And alders ring the bog, and bracken grows
        Beside it and birch saplings, or a willow
Raises huge arms ; there one might find repose
        In any place, with heather for a pillow.
        Some ancient lost thing, like an armadillo,
Might find a home there, so remote would seem
        From all the busy earth the heather's billow
That ripples in mild winds,, where mosses gleam
By pools that seem to touch earth's shores and those of dream.

52

Or sometimes, to remind one man is near,
    A track with ruts of little wheels may roam
Into the waste, where birches disappear,
    Past the last furze, till leprechaun or gnome
    Would seem more likely than what tread the loam
Of common fields ; and there the turf-stacks stand
    Like little houses of a curious home,
The scattered village of an elfin band,
Built under the full moon by some inhuman hand.

53

And grass and bracken on their roofs are laid
    To guard them from whatever storms may blow,
And birch-twigs lashed to them give further aid
    Against wet Autumns or December's snow.
    Some day in cottage fires these turfs will glow
Golden and orange, and down wind will ride
    Afar the curious scent that all men know
Who ever saw the Irish countryside,
In air and memory to linger and abide.

54   *November* 30

In the black bogs, the marshy lands with rushes
    Close to the square fields, now the floods lie deep,
For many a small stream down the ditches gushes
    To feed them in the valleys ; safely sleep
    The teal there now, and golden plover sweep
On sharp swift wings over those gleaming spaces,
    While slow across the sky appear to creep
Flocks of green plover, and now rumour traces
The wild grey geese, late seen in many neighbouring places.

55

Or, tired with wandering the upper air,
    The green and golden plover swoop along
The rushy marshes and then settle there
    And all together seem to sing one song,
    Or join in conversation, thousands strong,
Talking of matters that concern the wild,
    Trivial to us, as, to that golden throng,
Our high affairs, all lore we have compiled,
Are things to earth and stars and air unreconciled.

DECEMBER

          December 1

Now among days gone by sinks down November
    And floods still lie upon the lazy land
And, heavy upon Europe still, December
    Will see war lying, and the towns that stand
    Above it crumbling down like towers of sand
Builded by children that forget the tide.
    Remember, children, that along this strand
There will be tides again, as high, as wide.
Be not downcast to hear their coming prophesied.

2   *December* 2

Out of the West a colder wind to-day
    Is riding through the spaces of the sky,
Guiding those roaming flocks upon their way
    That travel the cloud-valleys bright and high
Whose calls we hear scarce louder than a sigh,
As to their far and unknown destinations
    Led by that wind and their own lore they fly ;
Or, leading them to their predestined stations,
It brings the ice and snow, and shapes the fates of nations.

3   *December* 3

The wind has veered a little and there blows
    Once more the Irish wind from the South-west
Bringing its rain by which the ivy grows,
    Nourishing moss and weeds and all the rest
    That conquer cottages and then invest
Towers of castles. And not only these
    Go down before the wind; the haughty crest
Of man's proud spirit bows with the tall trees.
This wind it is that brings us our neutralities.

The port of Antwerp opens.   That strange sight
   I saw once on the Rhine will show again,
White ensigns fluttering below the height
    Of Ehrenbreitstein.   Here the wind and rain
    Have taken the last leaves, but what remain
On one branch of a vine whose grapes are done,
    A bright but mournful wreath that shines in vain
Now that so far to southward goes the sun
To look on little hills where vineyards were begun.

5

To-day stood down the Home Guard, formed to hold
    The land against the host that never came,
Though many battles over us were rolled,
    When the sky blinked at night with sudden flame
    And white puffs showed by day our gunners' aim,
And battle and recruits' drill came our way
    Alternately.   Though she forget our name,
Yet, meeting Liberty, shall we not say
We stood beside her once, and in her darkest day ?

6   *December 4*

The wind, like some bird low along the flood,
    Ruffles the water with a passing wing
And the bare branches of the neighbouring wood
    Bow as he passes, eastward travelling
    On the dark pinions that are shadowing
Now the blue water, and now let it shine.
    Bright is the sky for the wind's wayfaring.
And omens are not easy to divine
But seem to hint of frost above the sun's decline.

7

Desolate seems the garden in these days,
    Empty of every fruit and every flower ;
Yet not quite empty, for from wilder ways
    Beyond the wall comes, in a quiet hour,
    A squirrel to the hazels, for the dower
He finds among the weeds below them shed ;
    Then slips back nimbly to his secret bower
Up by a pear-tree whose wide arms are spread
Along the wall, and thence to branches overhead.

Near to a village lies a bog, where geese
    Float on the water in flocks wild and free ;
And just beyond where the last rushes cease
    The tame geese dwell. How strange to each must be
    The line between them ! Do the grey lags see
What spell it was Man cast to make geese tame
    So that they dwell in houses as does he,
Where in his own house he guards even flame ?
And were the tame content, until the wild ones came ?

9

High in the West are cold clouds from whose cover
    Sometimes there comes a clear enchanted cry.
It is the wild note of the golden plover
    That in and out of the cloud-valleys fly
    And that towards evening are sailing high
Before they dip to the dark fields to sweep
    Over them in the night, like a great sigh,
And settle down upon the grass and sleep
Until dawn calls them up into the airy deep.

10

Wild weather with cold wind out of the west
    And all the floods that the wild weather brings
Seem to enlarge the space where wild things rest,
    Or where they sail and dance in airy rings :
    Storm is upon the side of untamed things
And aids them against Man, who by his fires
    Sits while they race on their world-wandering wings,
Singing the olden song of their swift choirs,
And draws his curtains shut before their last flight tires.

11

Now Greece, alas, fights Greece. Has not Bellona
    Supped long enough on Greek blood, at behest
Of Hitler ? O that some oak at Dodona,
    Some oracle, would warn them. Let her rest !
    She has dined well already. Her red nest
Should be in Prussia. Not where wait to bud
    Athenian flowers, for so long oppressed.
No more Barbarians pour out Greek blood.
And must the Greeks themselves mingle it with the mud ?

12

December 7

A sudden wonder past the window-pane
    Falls the first snow, the harvest of the high
Bright valleys that the golden plover gain
      When they go singing through them, as the sky
      Glows with the evening and their hundreds fly
In arrowy wedges ; this the omens told
    At sunset, when their portents prophesy
And red clouds give their messages to gold,
And clouds and winds and stars foresee the coming cold.

13

December 8

Cold hovers like a hawk about to slay,
    And in the North a threat of Winter's might
Seems to be uttered, as from far away
      And faintly : the blue sky is pale and bright,
      Across which clouds drift fiercely, the sun's light
Glaring upon their edges : wild things know
    What we but guess, gazing upon the height
Of these cloud-mountains ; they learned long ago
Which are the homes of hail and which of rain and snow.

14

December 9

The weather with which all the North was dark
    Is nearer to the earth, and puddles freeze.
On a cold wind the wandering birds embark.
      Still among dead leaves from the chestnut trees
      Two primroses are shining ; only these,
Strange exiles from their season, now remain
    Remembering Spring, and waking memories,
Among small creatures that the weeds contain,
Of warmer days which they foretell will come again.

15

December 10

The morning shows fields snowy and sky grey,
    And floods are ice : bare branches appear green
With lichens, which al. seasons see display
      Their verdure, and a golden willow's sheen
      Flashes among them : no more snow is seen
By noon, when Nature's mood seemed to have veered
    From frowns to a pale smile, and in between
Frowning and smiling all day she appeared,
While out of grey and into grey again Earth steered.

Now trees and grasses in the sunlight glow.
  The sky has that clear light the North wind brings,
And little clouds that cross it gleam as though
    They were rejoicing with all gleaming things,
    With high twigs, pigeons' breasts and seagulls' wings.
And once again the omens speak of frost,
    As the sun early to his setting swings
And under branches and low hills is lost,
While gold among the trees from his great store is tossed.

The jewels in Orion's belt last night
  Shone clearly, and low down among the trees
A large star glittered, and the rest were bright ;
  And a red sun this morning saw floods freeze.
  The sun goes upward but a few degrees,
Then sinks again and leaves the Evening Star
  To hold the western spaces, whence it sees
More frost preparing on our fields afar
And a few lands at peace, and many lands at war.

A gold sun rising where red clouds are curled
  Shines on white grass again.   Since was begun
This story of the wandering of the world
    Through its four seasons, half its course is run
    And it stands opposite, beyond the sun,
Heedless of all we heed, though in that time
    So much was freed, such victories were won,
That none will find material more sublime
Than this wild year of ours of which to make his rhyme.

Nature has changed her mood and looks at us
  From the South-west and all the frost is gone,
And those low clouds that are as numerous
    As Irish hills, which oft they rest upon,
    Have wholly filled the dome, where lately shone
The North wind in his brightness.   Now the sky
    Is low and unlit : all day on and on
There calls the plover's melancholy cry
As upon lazy flights from field to field they fly.

Like fairies, born on bright hills far from here,
    Chrysanthemums with all their sunny faces
Shine in our rooms, where silently they peer
    With one long stare at all the shadowed places,
    Trying to find there haply some lost traces
Of Summer, that is far upon its way
    To Africa's enormous gleaming spaces.
Golden and white and orange, trim and gay,
They brighten with their smiles the short December day.

21

December 15

Our lake has gone, all but a pool or two,
    Back into bygone ages, back to be
With fallen forests, old bogs long cut through
    And carried off in carts, a memory,
    A visitor of whom we only see
Faint traces in the grass.   The wild grey geese
    Are grazing near a bog, to which they flee,
When anyone disturbs the fields, for peace
Where reeds and rushes grow, and Man's fierce engines cease.

22

December 16

A rainy dawn, and far hills in its light
    Lift as from gold-mines under fairyland,
Then slowly fade, and soon are in our sight
    Only the thorns round fields we understand,
    With low clouds weighing down upon them, and
A South wind running through them bringing rain.
    Short is the day now, while on either hand
Night closes in, and the low sun in vain
Illumines earth awhile, then sinks in night again.

23

December 17

Among dead flowers and decaying weeds
    One lupin lingers in our garden yet.
Wholly alone it stands, as though it grieves
    Over the deathbeds of that brilliant set
    That were its comrades and can not forget
The shining faces that it used to know
    In days whose spirits like an old regret
Hover about the garden, moving slow
From lichen-covered trees to mouldering leaves below.

Southward, among low clouds now sinks the sun
   And scarcely rises over them at noon.
Over the meadows the green plover run.
    Snipe are in black bogs under a young moon,
    Where curlews whistle with their curious tune.
A man is ploughing where white seagulls measure
   Each yard he turns, with quick eyes, and as soon
As the plough passes they descend for treasure
Which Man from the deep earth has dug up for their pleasure.

Now against troops of the United States
   In Belgium and in Luxemburg are hurled
The hosts of those whom Liberty most hates
    And who hate Liberty. What smoke is curled
    Around them with what thunder ! While the world
Waits for the verdict, waits to hear if Mars
   Shall speak for freedom and his flag be furled,
Or whether it flap on and hide the stars
Till all mankind be crushed under his armoured cars.

A red-gold sunset and a pale-blue moon
   And golden plover flying past one horn ;
Green plover, with the light that dwindles soon
    Bright on their breasts, on winds of evening borne,
    Calling their clear calls, plaintive and forlorn ;
Seagulls to some far home for night returning,
   And jackdaws, with loud talk, to ruins worn
By centuries of ivy : these discerning,
I watched the western sky like flames of campfires burning.

Short is this twenty-first day of December,
   While the sun hides behind his curtains grey,
And Clio writes what ages will remember
    And battle rocks the nations far away.
    Clio will not concern herself to say
The golden plover to our fields are flying,
   Or partridges in rushy places stay,
Or care that geese go where tall reeds are sighing,
But stares with sombre joy to watch a million dying.

Anemones, forgetting where they are,
   Or haply seeing Greece in floral dreams
And waking, as their kindred wake afar
    By Parnees or by world-remembered streams,
    Bloom now by ones and twos ; a small bunch gleams
Beside me as I write, and memory
    Is led by them to Greece again, which seems
So friendly, that the Greeks' hostility
Sounds like some misheard tale of things that cannot be.

Now along picture-frames and shelves hangs holly
   Honouring Christmas and defending Man
Against the dark of the year's melancholy
    With the bright flash of its viridian
    And glow of its red berries, till we can
See by our firesides colour that is gone
    From all our fields ; there for a while we plan
To hoard the mirthful light that lately shone
On Northern lands whose hills it shines no more upon.

Around a pond beside a neighbour's lawn
   Stand golden willows at their loveliest,
Their leaves all lost, but, like a stormy dawn,
    Or sunset setting fire to all the West,
    Or else the fabled phœnix on her nest,
Their branches flame. Now, as the music blends
    With drone of planes upon their warlike quest,
The chapel of King's College, Cambridge, sends
Carols and other words of peace to the world's ends.

Now Christmas with its messages of peace
   And the world's answer, War ; as it has been
Till our days, when we dream that it will cease,
    We that have made more war than had been seen
    For ages ; yet our folly or our spleen
Are not to blame, for war and peace still go
    One after other as the sure, serene
Departing and returning of the flow,
At shorter intervals, of high tide and of low.

Yet bells of England, Scotland, Ireland, Wales
　　Ring out to-night from ether, chime on chime,
To give their peaceful message, that still fails
　　To mitigate the fury of our time.
　　Over the hills their echoes ring and rhyme,
Like a late wayfarer through wind and rain,
　　Bent on a steep track he can scarcely climb,
Who calls that he is lost, and calls again,
Although in the loud storm he thinks he cries in vain.

33　　　　　　　December 26

This is the day when Irish boys in bands,
　　In honour of St. Stephen or a wren,
But looking most for pence from friendly hands,
　　Go down the roads disguised as gnomes and men
　　And goblins, till they find a house, and then
They sing their songs and gather their reward.
　　Sometimes they dance, and many a citizen
Of great towns dances on the polished board
With far less skill than they on stone or the green sward.

34　　　　　　　December 27

The wind seems moving round towards the North,
　　And a white moon, near full, in a sky clear
Looks upon cold fields, upon which go forth
　　Only small animals that have no fear
　　Of cold, or need of fires, as we have here,
Who watch the gold flames dancing over logs
　　That lie on glowing embers, where the year
Warms its last days, and thereby men and dogs
Gather in close, and so forget the frost and fogs.

35　　　　　　　December 28

The sky and all the fields are bright to-day
　　And every stalk of grass is plumed with white.
At sunset a long arm of mist goes grey
　　Under the dark of woods, with ruby light
　　High in the upper branches : towards night
The grey mist rises higher, while still glows
　　A small high cloud, and the moon golden bright
Through a dark-lilac sky serenely goes,
And the mist steals more near, and still in stature grows.

Our garden by the magic of the frost
    Has grown white flowers over fallen weeds
And on the ruins of what Summer lost.
    The snipe no longer in his marshes feeds,
    And woodcock come to woods from furze and reeds.
Momentous in the sky the full moon gleams,
    For future liberties and laws and creeds
Depend on weather now, and moonlight seems
As potent in these days as any of Man's dreams.

37

Beautiful is that lonely orb of gold
    Wrecked by old craters, as we by our own
Are wrecking Earth. When it is dry and cold
    Haply more craters than what we have known,
    Pock-marking all Earth's features, will be shown
To distant watchers, that may learn thereby
    How by ourselves our world was overthrown
And how the might of our machinery
Left Earth the wreck they see still wandering through their sky.

A thaw is in the fields, though in the heather
    The frost still lies and moss is hard as clay,
And from the red bogs, driven by the weather,
    The snipe went lately and are still away
    Although the moon was full but yesterday,
Which calls them to the heather : now by streams,
    Till ice shall leave their mossy pools, they stay,
Seeking their food where running water gleams,
And uttering, as they rise, their shrill and curious screams.

The sun, as though cast down out of the height
    All day along the hills is reeling low.
Not yet we notice the increasing light
    Of his climb upward to the days that show
    The daffodils and to the times when blow
The hyacinths, and then the rose again,
    Far on the other side of sleet and snow.
Now of the old year but few hours remain,
Yet fraught, in such a year, with unknown loss or gain.

JANUARY

The old year in the night went raging hence'
   And raging in came nineteen forty-five.
Nature was calm, but for the vehemence
   Of her fierce offspring, Man, who seems to drive
   The old year out with fury ; that may thrive
The year his bells have summoned, which may be
   As furious as the last, and may survive
As long as it in mankind's memory,
Its gloomy scenes lit up at last by Victory.

Sometimes across the country goes a thrill,
   As a red coat shines and the hounds appear ;
And someone watches upon every hill,
   And rumour travels fast of fox or deer,
   And open are the doors of houses near ;
For an event is stirring, unrecorded
   Although it be for any future year,
Except where memories in old brains hoarded
Dwell upon ditches crossed, bars cleared and rivers forded.

The snowstorms that have roamed the Northern world
   Last night crossed Ireland, and the morning shines
White for a while, though soon the clouds are swirled
   Greyly south-east, and from the oaks and pines
   The snow slips down, but lingers in white lines
On cedars, then departs from grass and tree.
   For Ireland warmer than the lands of vines,
From which the snowstorms came, appears to be,
By some perplexing trick of our geography.

Now from the North the wind is riding sheer
    And all the climate that we know is gone.
Small clouds are shining in space blue and clear,
    Willows flash out, gold and vermilion,
    And sunlight brightens trunks of beech, whereon
Runs the tree-creeper like a mouse, where moss
    And lichen shine as bright as leaves have shone.
A kestrel with the sunlight on the gloss
Of his wing-feathers hangs in air and slants across.

Now buds of snowdrops show in sheltered places,
    A few emerging from their hoods of green,
And looking with demure and downcast faces
    Upon the flowerless and wintry scene,
    Like young girls in a ballroom where has been
No dancing yet, nor any music played,
    And few lights lit to make their merry sheen,
And there they wait, a small group in the shade,
And still no dancer comes to dance with any maid.

Still blooms a primrose by the chestnut tree,
    And three or four more could be gathered near,
Where winter frowns around them sullenly ;
    And, like a poet living in a year
    When none will hear his message, they appear ;
Or like small wayfarers that roam astray
    Along the circuit of the earth's career,
Looking for April, or for March or May,
And smiling brightly yet, though they have lost their way.

Clear are the constellations all, to-night ;
    And Venus, low and blue among the trees,
Is pouring out the glory of her light
    As though it glimmered from enormous seas.
    If mighty companies of orbs like these
Have any message we can understand
    It is to tell us that our floods will freeze,
And that Orion and his glittering band
Will twinkle all to-night on ice and frosty land.

Mountainous clouds of gold to eastward glow
    At evening with the sunlight from the West,
Mountains whose mines perhaps hold miles of snow.
    And, at the time the starling seeks his nest,
    All a rose-pink they glimmer, crest by crest.
The sun sets, and the face of Nature seems
    Like a bright smile that loses all its zest.
So turn to listlessness the rosy beams,
And the cold rises up and soon will grip the streams.

A mighty range of mountains southwards glides
    Again before us with its peaks bright gold,
Turning to crimson slowly while their sides
    Darken till there is nothing to behold
    Of their late glories, and in bitter cold
Pigeons and rooks go home through clear bright air.
    Hard as a city's pavements is the mould,
And all the omens seem to be aware
Winter is prowling South out of its Arctic lair.

Now blooms the ferny garden of the frost
    On window-panes, and all the grass is white.
The golden plover from the fields are lost.
    A seagull passes with its leisured flight,
    Bright as a planet in the outer night.
Sometimes a hawk sails over, the sun red
    On every feather of his pinions bright,
That still upon the lucid air are spread,
A kestrel watching where the fieldmouse hides its head.

A paper has a photograph displayed
    Of Mussolini marching in Milan
Slowly before some soldiers on parade,
    Held by the arm, and looking like a man
    Led by a spirit that had spread the span
Of its great wings and left him. So he goes
    With proud and vacant face, as though the plan
That the fierce spirit did to him disclose
Might even yet succeed ; how, he no longer knows.

A black frost grips the fields and a wind blows
    Out of the East, and the green plover cry
Plaintively, as they search new fields. Now goes
    The last snipe to the streams, and woodcock fly
    To thickest cover ; long since, travelling high,
The golden plover went to the sea-shore,
    And geese are gone where the long mud-banks lie
Among the tides, and rooks know by their lore
How many days of ice Dame Nature has in store.

To-day out of the ether Elgar spoke,
    As one with an immortal voice can do.
Clouds in our sky are low and dark like smoke
    Which the Northeaster wanders bleakly through.
    Logs burn on hearths where a thin flame or two
Flicker above a gold and ruddy glow
    That in this season shows a brighter view
Than the cold fields, where starving plover go
Under these ragged clouds that seem to threaten snow.

Bright on a window-sill a butterfly
    Sits with spread wings and gazes at the light
As though it wished to soar into the sky,
    Which it would do, rejoicing, if it might ;
    But the North wind would kill it before night,
And so, without the fuller liberty
    Beyond the pane, it dwells here till more bright
And higher shows the sun, and, when we see
The flowers shine again, it shall go wild and free.

Rumour has come that there have just been seen
    The buds of aconites, like small brass horns
That fairy trumpeters, arrayed in green,
    Far hence from now will blow on brightening morns
    To welcome Spring, what time she first adorns
The woods and fields. But she is far away
    Somewhere upon Sahara's northern bournes,
Just coming to the mountains, and our grey
Cold skies will not reflect her smiles for many a day.

Still shine chrysanthemums, the year's bright link
    Between the glory that October knew
And those days when the earliest buds will blink
    After their Winter's sleep, and skies turn blue
    Veiled by brief rain, which Spring comes smiling through.
Chrysanthemums, that seem like the year's dreams
    While sleeping in the cold, soon to come true,
When daffodils awaken her, and gleams
The kingcup in his pride along the banks of streams.

Now Clio with her old and intimate friend,
    Bellona, strides upon the Polish plain ;
And under cloudy skies near the world's end,
    Even here, the news has reached us, though the gain
    Is not for us to estimate : when wane
These days of ours, children will be taught
    The plans and daily march of that campaign,
And know how Liberty was homeward brought,
Unless she meet some doom that we have scarcely thought ;

Some doom in Poland, in a land of dooms.
    But past the thunder-glare of Victory
We cannot see how dark the future looms
    Beyond where Warsaw falls to Liberty,
    And Krakov, for a while at least, is free.
Here, on a South-west wind a shower of snow
    Falls, but it whitens neither grass nor tree.
Dark through the air like heavy feathers go
The large grey flakes, then shine awhile on fields below.

Bleak are these days while Earth awaits the Spring,
    And bleak indeed the days while Europe waits
For Liberty ; but some faint glimmering
    Hints sometimes Winter's bitterness abates,
    And Europe, that has watched so many fates
Overtake tyrants, sees the light that gleams
    Across the plains that Hitler devastates,
From Liberty returning by red streams
To Poland's valiant land, whereof so oft she dreams.

The world to-day appears a faint pale gold,
    And pale gold clouds drift eastwards in its sky.
Snow is in all the fields, and tree-trunks hold
    White drifts of it upon the sides that lie
    Bare to the West ; and, when the gold gleams die
With evening, another splendour glows
    And jade-green shines and turquoise in the high
Bright dome across which the great West wind blows
Towers and peaks agleam with orange, mauve and rose.

Nature, so secret in her ways, to-day
    Shows all her children's wanderings in snow ;
As though she let us see once in a way
    One page of the great book, which long ago
    She wrote upon the rocks, whose edges show
Sometimes in quarries, and which still she writes
    On grass and dew, so that the mornings know
The tale of all that happened in the nights.
And now the tale is plain even to our dull sights.

The pointed tracks of rabbits show how nigh
    They dared approach our solemn porticoes.
Neither respect for us nor their own shy
    Wild lore has kept them far as we suppose.
    On his five pads by pathways the dog goes.
Sometimes a hare has passed ; abruptly here
    A bird's tracks end and a short clear gash shows
Where a wing cut the snow ; slender and clear
Across the other tracks a fox's prints appear.

Or may be seen a cat's steps neat and round
    Where she has left the cushion and the fire
For the wild woodland and the frozen ground,
    For pussy can turn tiger at desire.
    Down on the world has now come Winter's ire.
We have had only omens hitherto.
    But now the frost has gripped the fields and, higher,
The twigs are standing white against the blue,
And pigeons go less high than they are wont to do.

24   January 23

Roads are all ice ; duck are in little streams ;
    A starling in the powdery snow lies dead ;
A mist has risen high and the sun gleams
    A disk of silver through ; cattle are fed
    With hay thrown down where the smooth snow is spread
Over all else ; rabbits look large and dark ;
    No birds are singing, and a hush is shed
Over a white world which, for all we mark,
Might be a world at peace ; and all the trees are stark.

25   January 24

Now upon all the branches, twigs and sprays
    Have bloomed the ferny crystals of the frost,
And light is from the ground, for in a haze
    The sun and the increasing moon are lost.
    The sky is grey, but where its arch is crossed
By any trees, whose pallid clusters stand
    Against the darkness like a wandering ghost
Upon the edge of night, as the command
Of cockcrow turns him back into the lone dark land.

26   January 25.

The haze has gone and now a golden light
    Touches the snow ; a gold tint pale like this
Glows all day long upon the pillars' white
    When sunlight touches the Acropolis,
    Which now sees Spring far off, but Winter is
Absolute here. Mallards with bright green heads
    On brown necks gather where the energies
Of small streams running from their pebbly beds
Keep a pond's end from ice, which all around them spreads.

27   January 26

Ice sheets the windows on the inner side
    And ice advances from the banks of streams,
To go one night perhaps with silent stride
    Right over them. Still Nature's white page gleams
    With countless stories on a thousand themes,
Written by small paws of wild wanderers there
    When all the woods awake and mankind dreams,
And one may read where went the fox and where,
To shelter from the cold, to the woods went the hare.

109

Blackbirds and robins have begun to die,
    And still the fields are hard and bright and cold.
Where lies a starling dead a rook walks by
    And pecks at it ; this is the time foretold
    By the bright wealth of berries, as some hold,
Which made the autumn hedges walls of red
    Below the glory of October's gold.
The moon, as rooks go home, with yellow head
Looks at the Evening Star, and Earth between them spread.

29

The world seems silent, while the Evening Star
    Goes blazing down through treetops in the West,
Silent and still, as though from fields afar
    It waited, hushed, for news, something unguessed ;
    So it lies half expectant in its rest
Under the moon, and shapes of ancient trees
    Stand like grey prophets, with dooms manifest
To them, that at this hour no other sees.
When shall Earth hear her foe is beaten to his knees ?

Mysterious forces in the deeps of Earth
    Crush common minerals to shapes of light,
Using, to make a diamond, the whole girth
    Of mountains, and each mineral in the night
    Of the deep earth follows its ancient rite,
Six sides for silica, for fluor four,
    And each according to its way ; but bright
Crystals of water, when the frost is hoar,
Surpass the fair design of all the mountains' store.

31

On all our windowpanes the crystals are
    Like ferns and flowers, silver, white and grey,
And some of them in shape are like a star,
    As fair as any in the Milky Way.
    What craftsman could invent such a display,
Let alone fashion it with gems or gold ?
    More starlings on the paths lie dead to-day,
And Winter now has Europe in its hold,
And even as Hitler's heart all Northern lands are cold.

Now the dead hush that for a week has lain
　　Over our fields has lifted and there blows
A wind from the South-east with snow and rain.
　　　A blackbird wears a look as though it knows
　　　A change is coming and an end to snows,
For on a wind such changes always ride.
　　　Low on the earth a grey sky seems to close,
And still the frozen snow lies bleak and wide,
And night comes chilly on and falls from every side.

The snow is gone, and starlings on the grass
　　Are finding food and know they have come through,
And rooks are happy, and the robins pass
　　　From post to post, looking as though they knew
　　　Their dreadful days are, over.　Now a few
Snipe have returned to marshes, where has gone
　　　The ice from water, but though lost to view
It still lies in the earth ; who walks upon
The marsh can feel it hard as when it lately shone.

The streams are full and brown and running fast,
　　And air is mild, and weakening is the cold
Grip of the frost upon the fields at last,
　　　Like an old curse remembered by the mould,
　　　As Europe still remembers Hitler's hold,
Clenched from the Caucasus to Channel Isles,
　　　Now like a tale of horror nearly told.
The Russians have advanced two hundred miles,
And Liberty at last, after long weeping, smiles.

35

So January passes, like the fall
　　Of Winter crashing stricken to the ground,
His hard grey armour split in fragments small
　　　Lying below the grass, while there resound
　　　Stories of how the Russian hosts confound
The power of the Tyrant, where they tether
　　　Their horses by the Oder and surround
Many a city.　What if Winter's weather
And Hitler's bitter rule soon rage away together !

III

FEBRUARY

1

Now February comes, that month whose fame
　　Is all unknown to us, though it shall be
Tremendous in far ages, like a flame
　　Burning upon a page of history,
　　Though what the writing there I cannot see.
And Hitler could not see it, long ago
　　When he attacked the Russians, and with glee
Urged on his armies, and forgot the snow.
And Prussia suffers now for all he did not know.

2

The snowdrops like a small folk that has been
　　In exile and is home from wandering,
In little companies may now be seen
　　At a grove's edge.　Mild breezes blow and bring
　　The snipe back to their marshes, where the Spring
Will find them soon.　And now the aconite
　　With its green hood that it has seemed to fling
Over its gold face looks up at the light
As though it smiled to see the end of Winter's might.

3

The golden plover to our fields again
　　Have come from where they sheltered by some shore
When ice was over all the inland plain,
　　And their clear note is in our sky once more
　　Where their swift lines of wandering pinions soar.
And hares have seen the Spring from far away
　　Or prophesied her coming by some lore
They have among them.　And dogs seem to play
More merrily in lanes than they did yesterday.

Winter has clutched the land with a last grip
   And frozen all the pools for a few hours,
Then spread his bitter wings again, while drip
   Down upon sheets of ice the melting showers.
   Rivers are sweeping by with increased powers,
Made mighty by a thousand fields of snow,
   Which melted in one day ; and the sky lours
With yet more rain, with which they soon will flow
More widely still, as snipe and curlew seem to know.

And now the earth feels sure of Winter's rout.
   This is a day whose shafts of sunlight streaming
Past trunks of trees brings the last snowdrop out
   And wakes the golden aconites from dreaming,
   With all their hoods thrown back, their faces gleaming
In every patch of sun. Young cabbages
   Peep from the ground where stand the old ones, seeming
To totter where they stand ; dark cypresses
Seem bright to-day, and bright the cedar's greeneries.

6

Now under glass the arum lilies blow,
   Which light in Africa the streams and vleis ;
And here stand primulas in pots arow ;
   And still chrysanthemums, which cheer the days
   That else were flowerless, flash back the rays ;
And cyclamens are blooming, which, where free,
   In Corsica shine now by all the ways.
And under dead leaves by a chestnut tree
One primrose greets the light that it has lived to see.

And still the streams run full, bearing away
   The water lately freed from Winter's hold.
Snipe are in wisps, as though awhile they stay
   In bands in which they travelled when the cold
   Drove them afar over the frozen wold
To distant streams. The mild South-west again
   Is blowing on our pastures as of old,
And ragged clouds that have let fall no rain
Gleam in the sun as they ride low across the plain.

While Death is reaping youth by German streams
    He does his work as ever over here
Among the calm and quiet, who, with dreams
    Less wild than once they were, await his spear
    By their own firesides : on this day I hear
News of an old friend's loss. She had the skill
    To tame all animals, which with no fear
Did as she bid them ; horses from the hill
Came where she beckoned, and were glad to do her will.

9

She was a poet too when she was young,
    Drawing her verses from the countryside,
And that untroubled calm where birds have sung
    Age after age, where simple things abide
    And simple folk ; and now that she has died
The world seems harder and the past more far,
    Lost beyond fields through which she used to ride,
And old years dwindle as a falling star
Receding from an age of noise and haste and war.

10

She dwelt near where the metre that I borrow
    First flowered, for they say the Faery Queen
Was written in those vales, where some must sorrow
    To-day for the wise heart and friendly mien
    Known to so many in that rural scene.
And as a girl she lived in lands as faery,
    By red bog and rich pasture, and, between,
The Galtee mountains rose up grey and airy
Gazing across the plains and woods of Tipperary.

11

The land is troubled, even in its sleep,
    By what is troubling every land and race,
And I can send no winter flowers to keep
    In memory old days which move apace
    Far from their little share of time and space.
So in a day all dark with Hitler's malice
    I offer these few verses in the place
Of wreath of flowers, like a silver chalice,
Holding not wine, but tears, graved with the name of Alice.

12   *February* 7

The German arms fight well before the walls
   Of Berlin, yet the world awaits the day
When that unbending power will break, as falls
    An elm that has long hidden its decay,
    Then crashes suddenly across the way
And lies there still. So at some unknown hour
    The thirteen evil years of Hitler's sway
Will pass into the dark, and there will flower
An era in their place led by some juster power.

13   *February* 8

Now here and there the shining crocus twinkles,
   And silver buds of willows are just out,
And the green hellebore and periwinkles
    Have posted each their most adventurous scout,
    And crowds of snowdrops glimmer round about ;
And sometimes from the trees at evening
    A twitter comes from birds that have no doubt
That only a few hills away is Spring,
Knowing the very vales where she is lingering.

14   *February* 9

Montgomery has moved again to-day,
   Who, when he moves, moves like the avalanche,
And German villages upon the way
    Of the attack that his divisions launch
    Begin to crumble ; far away, Avranches
Is now rebuilding, and the German turn
    Has come for screaming air, and skies that blanch,
As home Bellona comes. May what they earn
Teach them a way of Fate they were too slow to learn.

15   *February* 10

A touch of frost is on the grass and trees
   This morning, and at sight of it one thought
We all are thinking : will the Oder freeze
    And the last battle of Berlin be fought ?
    Here February's climbing sun has brought
Some snowflakes out, their graceful white skirts bright
    With pale-green patches, skirts that might be wrought
By fairy tailors working in the night
With strips of mist, and dew, and the moon's silver light.

These are yet few, but, where a glance may fall
    Suddenly upon snowdrops, they appear
Like an enchanted people wild and small
    That scamper through the sunlight from the sheer
    Darkness of trees, transforming, as they hear
A human footfall, to things motionless
    And silent, though still bright, in mid career.
So they stand still, and one can only guess
The rushing crowd's white feet, bright eyes and floating tress.

17

And hazels have put forth their catkins now,
    With here and there a little bright red bud,
As Spring from far away charms every bough
    And sends a little magic to the wood,
    Though not that full display which thrills the blood
In April, when the blackbirds chant together
    To greet the dawn, which rises with a flood
Of song, and every wing and every feather
Shines in the early light of April's sparkling weather.

Now driving rain sweeps past us, a grey sheet
    Beyond which Spring perhaps prepares to send
The crocuses to rise before her feet
    And tell that she will come from the world's end
    With daffodils and tulips, and will tend
The buds again upon the chestnut-tree,
    The beech-tree, then the oak-tree, and befriend
The growing lambs, and young things that are free
Through all the woods and serve not Man in slavery.

The sky is blue to-day and, swift and bright,
    Clouds race across it, from the South-west blown.
Gold aconites round tree-trunks come in sight
    Which, lately to their fullest splendour grown,
    Seem like a solid patch of sunlight thrown
Down on the grass.   And now the Lenten Roses,
    Rising above old moss and weeds, have shown
Their graceful bells ; and the new year discloses
The purple crocus, that among the grass reposes.

The lichen on a little shrub is lit
    With starry bloom that has flashed out to-day :
Pale golden stars with four points shine on it,
    Tiny as any in the Milky Way.
    And, like a spark of Indian sky astray,
In sheltered places glory-of-the-snow
    Looks up with its six petals, which display
A hope of Spring, as far away may blow
The bugles of free men beyond a ruling foe.

Now a few buds of nectarines appear
    Where glass has made for them a house of dreams,
Wherein they dream of France ere Spring is here,
    When all the sunny southern country seems
    A shining paradise by earthly streams.
Still blooms the winter jasmine on a wall,
    Whose yellow flowers shone in the pale beams
Of January's sun and saw the fall
Of the old year and will shine on till blackbirds call.

A wind is moaning loudly in old towers.
    And much it has to mourn for, if it cares
Ought for the race of Man ; for in these hours
    Man's enemy, in his retreat, prepares
    The last of all his stratagems and snares,
Haply the worst, because he has not long.
    Meanwhile the land of his misruling glares
By night with the avenging of the wrong
He did so gleefully to us when he was strong.

Now dark leaves flash more bright in shrubberies.
    And now green buds on currant-bushes show
And just the tips of buds on gooseberries ;
    And red anemones in gardens glow ;
    And, sheltered from the North, some bee-flowers grow,
Surprising Winter, if it still be here,
    Though birds and buds and squirrels seem to know,
Whatever be the date, that Spring is near
And Winter soon will be, like Hitler, an old fear.

From a deep tree I heard a thrush unseen
    Singing to say that Winter-time is over,
Singing perhaps that grass will soon be green,
    That primroses will come, and then the clover,
    And home to nests again go every rover.
Soon will that song from all the hedges ring.
    And on his way by Irish roads the drover
Will move by choirs of thrushes, heartening
His lonely journey with the symphony they sing.

Last night a stag, escaped from the Ward Hunt,
    In the last light appeared as ghosts appear,
A shape before our windows, close in front
    Eating the grass, with ever-listening ear,
    As though on tiptoe, ready, should he hear
The least alarm, to spring into the speed
    That showed in every step, like something near,
But sleeping, to be wakened wide at need.
So, like a race-horse at the post, we saw him feed.

Now, like an orchestra about to play,
    The blackbirds tune their flutes at evening,
When, like a waterfall from far away,
    The murmur of the rooks is heralding
    The earlier stars, and home from wandering
Passes the heron by the way he takes
    At every nightfall : not as yet they sing
As when in April their wild music breaks
At dawn upon the woods, and all the world awakes.

Daphne's pink flowers among crimson buds
    Are showing now, and now the celandine
Peers out from hedgerows and the edge of woods,
    And crocuses in golden clusters shine ;
    And now some foreign heath has shown a sign
Of waking in its exile, from the sleep
    That it has slept all through the sun's decline,
And here and there a bloom begins to peep ;
And rhododendrons still within their green buds keep.

Like a new comrade at a merry dance,
    Among the snowdrops now the crocus gleams ;
And the first daisy rises ; a bright glance
        She gives from smiling features, as it seems ;
        And violets awaken from long dreams,
Where an old oak gives shelter, but a few ;
        Not like that splendour that by Grecian streams
A while ago in one great carpet grew
Under Apollo's home in gardens that I knew.

29

Greener the moss upon the feet of oaks,
    And brighter the green circles on the beech,
Which lichen makes upon the grey-green cloaks
        That seem to drape the mighty limbs of each.
        The delicate pink blossom of the peach
Is looking from its windows, and outside
        The mauve-green leaves of lupins, that now reach
Only an inch or two from earth, provide
A setting for the dew sparkling with diamond's pride.

And, blue as fragments of a southern sky,
    Grape-hyacinths are stealing into sight
In ones and twos ; and flowerbeds now lie
        No longer wholly bare, though not yet bright ;
        For coloured primroses, blue, mauve and white,
Have come to dwell there, before their wild kin
        With lovely fairy-faces yet delight
The dells under the beech, though there begin
One or two pale-gold scouts of theirs to lurk therein.

31

The red anemones are at their best ;
    The leaves of tulips from the earth arise ;
The catkins of a willow shine with zest,
        White as a fountain flung against the skies ;
        An early rhododendron, to surprise
Retreating Winter, flashes out one flower,
        And under glass there glows before our eyes
An amaryllis huge and red, the hour
Come when its beauty reigns with all its magic power.

A moon half full, and one day more, to-night
    Peers through a horde of racing clouds that go
Like spirits past it, casting round its light
    A halo that their riders seem to throw,
    As they sweep by and, in their passing, glow.
And through the ether comes the melody
    Debussy wrote upon the ebb and flow
And thundering and smiling of the sea.
Thus music rides the sky with clouds for company.

                        February 22

The red anemones are all asleep
    After a shower, and the birds are singing
As though the peach-blossom had seen Spring peep
    Over the garden wall where they are winging
    And told the news, and whispered she was bringing
All that the blackbirds dream. And robins see
    That distant charm which sets the first buds springing.
I saw one close, upon a little tree,
And that, with his small words, was what he said to me.

34

Like palms upon the coast by Zanzibar,
    Shapely but shrunken, by an airman seen
At sunrise from the void above them far,
    The leaves of monkshood show their brilliant green,
    Palm-like, and last year's foliage lies between.
Now under beech, in shelter of a hill,
    As the first planet shows in the serene
Which the unnumbered stars are soon to fill,
There flashes into sight the earliest daffodil.

35

And where the little Skane by hartstongue runs
    And mossy rocks, are many buds that wait
To break into the bloom that March's suns
    Will gild until their crowds illuminate
    The shadows of the woods, to stay as late
As the last swallow's advent, and to hear
    The blackbird's call at dawn reverberate,
Making a golden threshold for the year
To walk through from the wastes of Time into our sphere.

Each day the moss grows brighter on the roots
 Of aged trees. The leaf on rambler-roses,
Elders and honeysuckles brightly shoots ;
 And buds on rhododendrons show their noses,
 The pale pink kind whose flower first uncloses,
And ribes buds are out ; and fairy gold
 Shines on the hazels where the light reposes ;
And chestnut-buds are sticky, which enfold
One of the fairest sights the swallows will behold.

37

Minute upon the thorn, scarce to be seen,
 The buds peep out where all was dark so long,
Pink specks among faint streaks of palest green
 Lured from their sleep by the first blackbird's song.
 And now we hear the Turks against the wrong
Of Hitler take up arms. With what delight
 Shall we not welcome those men tall and strong
To be our allies and help put to flight
That tyranny which darkened Europe with its night.

In his warm house the cineraria glows,
 Surpassing any silks or paints of ours,
His colour, now that we forget the rose,
 Brighter than all the light in other flowers
 That shine beside him in their little bowers,
Except the amaryllis, that like Mars
 Flashing out red among the heavenly powers
Scorns all the gentler lights of other stars,
Which pale, as arts of peace pale here before his wars.

Where once a lime was cut thin saplings rise
 In a thick cluster with red buds at ends,
And periwinkles open their blue eyes,
 And out into the world a thorn-tree sends
 A few green leaves, and from the grass ascends
A primrose here and there, and glints the gold
 Now where the daffodil's bud earthward bends.
And blue No-never shines as though the cold
Were gone and Winter were far to the Arctic rolled.

Titmice are singing on an apple-bough
　　With bullfinches, and in a misty rain
The aconites have shut their blooms, and now
　　The red anemones are closed again.
　　Overgrown daisies from the garden strain
A nourishment their wild kin do not know ;
　　Pink rhododendron buds to flowers attain ;
Green berries on a spotted laurel grow,
And under glass the heads of gay carnations show.

41　　　　　　　　　　　　　　　*February 26*

In purple cloaks and wearing small gold crowns
　　A company of crocuses appears;
And still the snowdrops spread their satin gowns,
　　And a white violet awaking hears
　　The thrush's song, as February nears
Its violent end, deciding which shall be
　　The guide of mankind for a hundred years,
From here to Yokohama, Liberty,
Or, as still Hitler hopes, the curse of tyranny.

42　　　　　　　　　　　　　　　*February 27*

Below a pale-green pyramid of buds
　　A bloom of berberis is all agleam
Underneath chestnut-trees, by which there floods
　　The shadowed water of a little stream.
　　Soon by its banks the daffodils will teem :
Nearly a hundred are already there,
　　Drooping their golden heads, and many seem
About to break from bud in the mild air,
And small birds out of sight are singing everywhere.

43

A yellow powdered bloom is on the yew,
　　And little leaves on shrubs begin to show ;
　A cypress seems to flash with brighter hue ;
　　A thuja stands unchanged, but for the row
　　Of ochre seed-pods on each twig, which glow
No longer, but are empty now and brown ;
　　The aconites are dim, as though they know
The time has come to lay their splendour down
When the first dandelion lifts his golden crown.

The gorse, that all months know, has seen the Spring
    Far off beyond dim mountains, whose serene
Blue slopes conceal her from our questioning,
    And elders see what we have not yet seen
    And stretch their leaves to welcome the year's queen,
And lilac leaves peer from a city's square,
    And all in bloom above their brilliant green
One cherry lifts a splendour in the air,
Making the sky above, and bricks behind, more fair.

45

So February, having seen afar
    Light shining from Spring's footsteps on the hills,
And having seen, as vivid as a star
    Flashing from darkness, that clear light that fills
    Heaven above and dances in the rills,
Which goes before the feet of Liberty,
    Now leaves us, with her gift of daffodils.
And March approaches Earth, whose days shall be
A period to awe the Muse of History.

MARCH

Green hellebore, that strange and lovely flower,
    Like leaves enchanted, is now fully blown.
Now frogs begin to spawn, and in that hour
    When the first star is only newly shown
    Some watcher, standing quiet as a stone,
May see a pair of woodcock on their way
    To feed in marshes, from a dark wood flown.
And coltsfoot's fluffy flowers, gold and grey
In dank land under trees, shine in the cold bright day.

2

To-day the peach-blossom is in its prime,
    Its beauty gleaming on the sunny wall.
The pale-pink petals in a few hours' time,
    To-night perhaps, will flicker to their fall.
    One blossom of Forsythia hears the call
Of Spring ; and Orcuba, the spotted laurel,
    Reddens its berries ; and the birds are all
Awaiting Spring, as though Man's deadly quarrel
Were a tale told far off with neither point nor moral.

3

Shadows are white this morning, for a frost
    Has ridden the North wind ; the feet of Spring
Are checked by it, but hills that she has crossed
    Are still behind her, and her journeying
    Is t'wards us yet, although now lingering ;
And this a solitary pigeon cries,
    As one voice of a sentry challenging
May tell where in the night an army lies,
About to strike, perhaps, at wintry tyrannies.

4

Now the white army of the snowdrop droops,
    Weary with standing against Winter's might,
And primroses steal out like fresher troops
    That reinforce with victory in sight,
    With daffodils upon their left and right.
White buds appear on the laburnum trees
    And withered is the golden aconite,
Though more and more among the grass one sees
The celandine's bright face, waiting for April's bees.

5

And still retreating Winter's sword of ice
    Is drawn by night, and Spring's advance is slow.
Yet, where a garden's sheltered ways entice
    A primrose from the wild to come and grow
    Under an apple-tree, its blossoms show
Abundantly among the primmer flowers
    And smile with upturned faces, though there blow
The bitter winds of Winter's final hours
Which slew the aconite among its little bowers.

6

Now one by one, like stars at evening,
    Pink blossoms on the prunus trees appear
And dog's-tooth violet is shimmering
    Above its mottled leaves, and we can hear
    Lambs bleating in the fields, and in a sheer
High tree a heron has her mighty nest,
    And over it her circling pinions steer
(When wanderers in the wood disturb her rest)
Floating upon a strong cold wind out of the West.

7

The Ward to-day came gaily to our wood
    To hunt their outlier, that drank last night
Out of a stream and left his tracks in mud.
    For half an hour they made our fields more bright,
Then passed like distant thunder out of sight
With Meath spread out before them, where I rode
    After the fox, the stag and hare by light
Of other years, when Percy Maynard showed
Good sport and when with us John Watson still abode.

Rooks in the fields are walking with an air,
    And jackdaws watch the chimneys, as a man
Going to marry may watch houses where
    Flats are to let.   To-day the snipe began
    High up in evening's still caerulean
That curious note which over heath and ling,
    With their tail-feathers outspread like a fan
Against the air, they make the wind to sing
As they fly headlong down, and thus they greet the Spring.

9   *March* 8

The silver fountain of a willow's bloom
    Turned gold to-day, and now like stars appear
Mirabelle blossoms bright against the gloom
    Of the dark trunk, and primulas grow near
    And polyanthus ; but the bloom is sere
On the pink rhododendron, that too soon
    Looked out, believing that the Spring was here,
And only found a frost under the moon
And withered in the dawn, hearing no blackbird's tune.

10

Where a low hill gives shelter from the North,
    And under boles of oaks and chestnut-trees,
White violets in multitudes come forth,
    Scenting the skirts of every passing breeze,
    And here and there the shadows on the leas
Are lit by their blue comrades ; and the glow
    Of daffodils increases, and with these
Shine primroses and glory-of-the-snow,
And periwinkles now by lawns and pathways blow.

11

Rising above the long roar of the rooks
    At evening one hears the thrushes' song
Filling the woods until the leafy nooks
    Are nearly dark, and beetles rush along
    Humming their insect-music clear and strong ;
And small things make swift ripples in a stream,
    Though nothing shows of all the shapes that throng
A wood at nightfall but the ripples' gleam,
While water seems to wake and all the land to dream.

A new voice sang to-day, and as I stood
    Under a willow tree that seemed to stray
Into the light a little from a wood ;
    And all its blooms were brightening the day ;
    High in its golden haze, like fountains' spray
At sunrise, I could hear the sound of bees,
    And, droning through their song upon his way
To gather honey, sometimes down the breeze
A bumblebee came by with louder note than these.

13

A pigeon from a deep green cypress flies
    A little way, then watches from an oak.
We from our houses do not have to rise
    So suddenly and flee.   Yet, since there broke
    This war on us, the swift and sudden stroke
On the long battlefield from York to Kent,
    By which our foes would have imposed their yoke,
Has taught us something of the wild lives spent
On watch all day and night with danger imminent.

And now the berberis puts out its leaves
    In little clusters beside every thorn,
With scarlet buds ; and where a plum receives
    The early sun its young pale shoots adorn
    A garden wall. Now, walking in the morn,
A water-wagtail on the gravel goes
    Near to a wall where ivy all unshorn
Has given shelter against Winter's snows
And soon will fill with nests, as every wagtail knows.

15

Squirrels in pairs may often now be seen
    Laughing round pine-trunks, and the golden faces
Of all the daffodils now southwards lean,
    Watching the sun go by their sheltered places ;
    And laurestinus shows the dark pink traces
Of buds that will break out in blossom soon.
    And now with dwindling horns from starry spaces
Into the morning there has gone the moon.
And every evening grows more clear the thrushes' tune.

Now privet from its wintry slumber rouses
    By roadsides, where grey circles sometimes show,
Left by the men that never enter houses,
    Old campfires of the tinkers ; and a glow
    Is on the gorse, and chickweed's flowers grow,
And shepherd's-purse again ; and here and there
    Green flashes from one thorn-tree in a row.
And jackdaws' nests are·built in trees still bare,
But knowing, every tree, that Spring is in the air.

17   March 12

Now winter-heliotrope's fat weed is seen
    With folded buds below the starry bloom ;
The glory of a weeping-willow's green
    Exults against the last of Winter's gloom,
    And early petals shine upon the broom.
And now Forsythia is a golden light,
    And Spring is shining, though behind her loom
The horrors of a world snatched back from night,
And redly flows the Rhine with its tremendous fight.

18   March 13

Now blue anemones have raised their faces,
    And blooming still is glory-of-the-snow,
And daffodils shine on in sunny spaces.
    And primroses in woods are all aglow,
    And violets beneath the beeches blow,
And ribes like a sunset after thunder
    Gleams ruddy-pink where oak and cypress grow
And celandines and daisies shelter under,
And small birds greet the Spring with an increasing wonder.

19   March 14

Over each bunch of Daphne's crimson flowers
    Young leaves in bright green clusters now appear ;
And now peep out to look for sunny hours,
    Which the North wind has blown away from here,
    Grape-hyacinths, and in a garden near
Aubretia lifts her bright mauve face to smile
    Along a border.   Gold and scarlet clear
Shine on a goldfinch, and small songs beguile
The listener, and Spring's buds are breaking all the while.

Now flat upon the ground the leaves of thistles
    Show their fresh green under a haze of grey,
And curlews give their short, repeated whistles,
    Unlike that call that on an Autumn day
    Drifts from some wanderer upon his way
From sea to marsh over the Irish hills.
    This is the mating-call, with which they say
That Spring is here, before the blackbird trills
Or their full glory glows upon the daffodils.

21

And saxifrage on its deep carpet grows
    In gardens, and beside it arabis ;
And small leaves peep upon the rambler rose,
    The honeysuckle and the clematis ;
    And tits and robins sing their melodies.
But in the distant air is throbbing now
    The sound Man makes with that grim friend of his,
That sombre spirit which our times allow
To take the horse's place and drive afield the plough.

A nectarine out-of-doors is all in bloom
    Against a wall, and by its deep blush show
White petals of a cherry and a plum.
    Mirabelle blossomed some ten days ago
    And still enchants the passer-by, although
The bullfinches upon its petals feed
    Or scatter them upon the ground. A glow
Is on the larch, and a few green buds, freed
From Winter, peep to see if Spring is here indeed.

Sycamore, lime and whitebeam are in bud,
    And on a chestnut a few leaves unfold ;
But oak and ash are naked in the wood,
    And beech has heard no word of what is told
    Of Spring's arrival. In the sunlight's gold
A butterfly is dancing on the air
    Over the early flowers, for the cold
Is gone which kept him in his leafy lair
Hidden, asleep, till signs of Spring are everywhere.

A wind is riding through the sky to-day
    And, as we watch for new leaves to appear,
The leaves of last year dance again and stray
    Like ghosts that have been called up from the bier
    By some catastrophe that shakes our sphere,
Such as now reddens Oder and the Rhine
    And levels ancient cities, but brings near
The end of tyranny.   More thorn-trees shine
And small leaves under glass appear upon a vine.

25

Again those murmurs through a cloudy sky,
    That come so rarely here, above us go ;
The sound of some that rescue Liberty,
    Or hate her ; which they be we cannot know.
    And what of her ? How looks she when her foe
Goes past her ? Does the goddess turn her head ?
    Does some faint interest in the deep eyes show,
Which never look on us, as though instead
Of being neutrals, proud of that choice, we were dead ?

The glow upon the larch is turning green,
    And green are hedges, and small buds are white
Upon the blackthorn, and there may be seen
    The bloom of willow with its golden light
    Shining upon the roadside.   Out of sight
To-day are all the hills that look on Meath,
    For rain has hidden them, and every height
Is gone, and in their place the low clouds wreathe
Flat fields on which the sighs of winds from ocean breathe.

27

To-day the point-to-point of the Meath Hunt
    Brought out bright silk to glitter once again
Through fields of farms that lie upon the front
    Of a long slope, beyond which lies the chain
    Of little mountains hidden by the rain,
But often shining with a faery glow
    From their calm haunts across the rich green plain.
Here gather all that love sport or that know
By rumour or by eye which horse is built to go.

Now all the blue anemones are blown
   On tended land, not garden and not field,
Where shrubs give shelter and tall trees have grown
     Through the long ages given to the weald,
     So that one tree sees things that are revealed
Only to dynasties, to pass away
     With empires, falling when a crown has reeled,
And far outlasting all who proudly say
They own what stood before, and will survive, their day.

29

And there the daffodils, now waves of gold,
   Give sunlight to the shadows, and wood-sorrel
Begins to peep where sheltered from the cold
     By an old hornbeam's roots near groves of laurel
     And berberis, whose berries are bright coral
When autumn comes, and now is just in bud ;
     And all cock-pheasants have begun to quarrel,
Calling at evening for each other's blood
With loud triumphant notes resounding from the wood.

Now primroses to their full glory grow
   Under the beechwoods, amber pools of light ;
And wild anemones begin to show,
     But sparsely here, not as upon the height
     Of Kentish downs where thousands come in sight
Under the hazels in the early Spring,
     Whose beauty I remember with delight,
Downs over which the guns were thundering
When Hitler's wildest hopes were strong upon the wing.

Pyrus Japonica beside a wall
   Is glowing with its gaudy alien flower,
And all the petals of the peaches fall ;
     And from the nectarines a deep-pink shower
     Has gone long since, and they await the hour
Of ripening fruit ; and the first cowslip comes.
     And lungwort shows in beds ; and Eisenhower
Seizes the Rhine, and there Death sits and drums,
While here a wandering bee among vine-tendrils hums.

Tortoiseshells and anemones together
　　By garden paths are shining in the sun,
And bloom on elms is gold in the bright weather,
　　And green is on the larch, if only one,
　　And further from their homes the rabbits run,
And leaves upon a mountain-ash are breaking
　　Green as a meteor ; and is now begun
A stir in woodlands, as of dryads waking,
And Spring steps soft, as though all Europe were not shaking.

Now white narcissi from a beech-tree's shadow
　　Look out upon the blue anemones
Where daffodils have made an El Dorado
　　In sunlight slipping by the trunks of trees.
　　A large gold daisy attracts bumblebees
And from a crack in a high garden wall
　　Ivyleaf-toadflax has peeped out and sees
The fresh white blossom on the plum.　And all
The cherry is in bloom, and thrushes call and call.

A ladybird upon the grey-green leaves
　　Of a sea-buckthorn shows her speckled red ;
And one blue speedwell wakens and believes
　　That Spring is come, as all the birds have said ;
　　And sycamores are out ; and, not yet spread,
But green, a hornbeam's little leaves are shining ;
　　And clouds before a wind ride overhead
With sunlight all a-dazzle in their lining ;
And crocuses are dead and daphne's bloom declining.

And damsons are all dressed in dainty white,
　　And dark red catkins on the poplars show,
And on the elm-trees leaves are just in sight,
　　And bloom is on the box, a tiny glow
　　Among dark foliage.　And now a row
Of apple-trees has broken into leaf,
　　And leaf is on the rose.　And now as though
Blue eyes smiled gladly, after sleep or grief,
Forget-me-nots look up.　And frosts are rare and brief.

36

Now hazels change the glow their catkins made,
    And the young leaf above their lichen gleams,
And far away they look like some grey shade
    Such as may hang at evening over streams,
    Lit faintly by the late and level beams ;
And to syringa and laburnum come
    The young green leaves, as though long wintry dreams
At last came true ; and all about a plum
The bees are gathered now, singing in one long hum.

37

And now a green mist glitters on the larch,
    And golden on the dogwood is the light
Of its new foliage. The month of March
    Has brought us Spring, and brightened the long night
    That lay on Europe, till there comes in sight
The face of Victory beyond the Rhine,
    Though partly veiled with smoke of the last fight,
Not smiling yet on the advancing line,
But guiding it through wreck of town and field and vine.

38   *March* 27

A deep-mauve pea among the grasses creeps
    In an old garden, and a cloud of gold
Hangs on a chestnut sleeping as one sleeps
    With dawn upon his face, who can behold
    Both dreams and daylight : even now unfold,
On other chestnut-trees the lovely leaves.
    And now through all the woods the news is told
That Spring is here, although the oak receives
No word of it, nor ash, and the beech scarce believes.

39   *March* 28

Now in the hedges' new and brilliant green
    The blackthorn flashes out in all its glory,
White clusters on dark stems, that may be seen
    Where under sun and cloud the mountains hoary
    Look over Leinster's grassy territory.
And now from woods the wild and piercing note
    Some blackbird utters, urged to tell his story
By Spring's sheer magic, will through evening float,
Like one word of a spell from an enchanted throat.

A golden willow shines, and what was gold
    Is now a flame.　And now the pale mauve flowers
Of rosemary are out ;　and now unfold
    The petals of the pear.　No more the powers
    Of Winter trouble any field of ours :
They have gone northwards where the wild geese go.
    And sun is on the skirts of little showers,
And green is every thorn and mild winds blow,
And daffodils in all their utmost glory grow.

Now seagulls whiten patches of a field
    Noisily harrowed, and sometimes a rook
Drops down to see what the turned earth may yield ;
    And every shrub that shelters every nook
    Is now in leaf ;　and early blossoms look
Out from a sycamore, all drooping down
    Under the copper leaves.　What fancy took
Spring, of all places, first into a town,
Where Dublin wears her hills about her like a crown ?

For first I saw the sycamore bloom there
    Before the country saw its gold appear,
And earlier I saw a Dublin square
    With cherry-blossom bright, while gardens near
    Showed weeping willows brightening the year
With new green leaves, and laurestinus shone
    Before one bud of it had opened here.
Now Spring over the plain of Meath has gone
Illuming all the land that Tara looks upon.

Now like a green moth fresh from its cocoon,
    Hanging its brilliant wings before they fly
Upon long journeys underneath the moon,
    The chestnut leaf hangs limp against the sky,
    Lovely though not yet spread, and somewhere nigh
The earliest hyacinths are just in flower,
    Peering round trees, among the shadows shy,
As though they hid from some unfriendly power.
And trailing through the fields goes March's final shower.

APRIL

1

Not even rain can hinder April's glow ;
   For the thorn flashes with its blazing green,
And seeds upon a distant elm-tree show
   Like sunrise on gold mountains, and the sheen
   On poplar-leaves is orange, and between
Leaves and unfolding buds there is a light
   Upon the chestnuts, as though Spring were seen
Dawning upon the world, out of the night
Beyond us, wherein she so long was lost to sight.

2

Lo, Spring was walking lately in this wood,
   And from her footsteps the ground-ivy twinkles
Lighting the shade wherever she has stood.
   And through the wood a stream that the wind wrinkles
   Spotted with drops that a light shower sprinkles
Runs slowly by. Upon the evening air
   A chapel bell across the valley tinkles
And greyer grows the sky, yet everywhere
The green and gold of Spring's enchantment flash and flare.

3

Now dandelions on a garden wall
   Flash as the sunlight passes over it,
Lighting a golden cypress up, and all
   The blossom of a pear, although it lit
   These flashes for a moment while there flit
The clouds of April close upon its gold.
   And now a peacock gives the benefit
Of his great splendour, as his plumes unfold
In gleaming green and blue that all his hens behold.

And now the leaves flash out upon the lime,
    Light green, and holding sunlight every one ;
And oak and ash and beech still bide their time,
    And all the rest are shining in the sun ;
    And full with April's showers small streams run.
And while the sunlight widens on the world
    Liberty lifts the shadow that the Hun
Lay cold on Europe, as his hosts are hurled
    East from the Rhine, and West from the red flag unfurled.

5

And golden-saxifrage is shining now,
    A glow among the grass as bright as flame,
Like a green meteor on the morning's brow.
    And one more tree beside the ones I name
    Is leafless still, the chestnut that lays claim
To Spanish lineage, its sombre shape
    Glooming like some old ogre dark and lame
Among the merry elms and limes that drape
Their limbs with the green gold of April's cloak and cape.

6   *April 3*

Now flares the elm against a sky made grey
    By one of April's wild and wandering showers,
Like flash of sunlight that has lost its way,
    To be entangled in this world of ours
    Instead of passing on to light the bowers
Of distant constellations, sunlight streaming
    On this side of the clouds from golden towers ;
For nothing brighter than the elm is gleaming
Till the laburnum wakes, with lilac, from their dreaming.

7

To-day the white dead-nettle's blooms appear,
    Like groups of snakes' heads lifted up to smite,
From every pair of leaves ; and, shining clear
    Against a dark wood, lilac leaves are bright.
    Now squirrels from the tips of branches bite
The shoots of chestnuts. This year's beeches show
    Like butterflies that on the soil alight
With two wings, green above and white below,
The forest that would reign after Man's overthrow.

A dark red rhododendron starts to flower,
    And from mown grass the daisies lift their faces ;
And jackdaws are disturbed in an old tower
    Because men clip the ivy, that encases
    Haunts that belong to them and kindred races,
As they suppose and as their forbears taught.
    As we should feel if curtains, blinds and laces
Were from our houses by a wild wind caught,
So jackdaws may regard this ruin they see wrought.

9

And now the laurel's scented bloom is seen
    On upper branches where it gets the sun,
And the white birch has thrown its scarf of green
    About it, and the aspen has begun
    To wave pale leaves ; and, breaking one by one,
The buds of laurestinus turn to flowers ;
    And under hazels where slow waters run
The kingcup twinkles in his golden bowers,
One of the brightest lights of April's earlier hours.

The first white butterfly was out to-day,
    And two white tulips, and a single oak
Flashed with a bunch of leaves ; and all the way
    Along a road the shining blackthorn broke
    Through the green hedge, or like a cloud of smoke
Lifted above it, while more like a flame
    The foliage of poplars has awoke,
With light of Lombardy, from which they came ;
And anthems of the birds are praising April's name.

11

And now the daffodils begin to die,
    Though thousands with the golden flag still flying
May live to see the swallows in our sky,
    If they come soon from where the shells are sighing
    Over towns desolate and armies dying,
Unhurt by all the warfare that Man wages,
    Haply remembering, where his homes are lying
Under the howitzer's tremendous rages,
Only that Man is he who has invented cages.

12

The Spring's enchantment and the shining air
    Have brought a few more tulips out to-day ;
More daisies dot the lawns ; and in the pear
    The song of bees is louder, where they stray
    Over the mass of blossom. What a way
To earn one's living ! Working amongst flowers,
    Not as men work for jewels dark in clay,
But seeking treasure through the sunny hours
Where the sweet gold is stored in April's loveliest bowers.

13

Now trees are full of music from unseen
    Small singers, and the earth is bright with gold
Of daffodils and primroses, and green
    With leaves of the wood-sorrel, whence unfold
    The delicate mauve flowers and behold
Forget-me-nots all round and violets.
    And now indeed the dark days and the cold
Are over, for with airy minuets
A hawk-moth sways above a pear-tree's flowerets.

14

And now the very flag I once saw fly
    From Ehrenbreitstein flies from it again,
The very same flag under the same sky,
    Taken from where some thought it would remain
    In Washington, once more into the rain
And wind and whatsoever storms may blow
    Along the Rhine ; and all will blow in vain
Against that flag, whether of sleet or snow
Or whether those red storms that German pastures know.

15   *April* 7

And now hedge-parsley blooms beside the road,
    And leaves of silverweed begin to gleam,
And yesterday the first mauve milkmaid showed,
    And more are out to-day, and by a stream
    The kingcups are still shining, and a beam
Of sunlight touches here and there the petals
    Of the wild strawberry, and blackbirds seem
Still more triumphantly to show their mettles,
As down upon the woods the hush of evening settles.

16

Bremen to-night, before its fortunes founder,
    Tells us that fighting is a thing not done,
That who should still make war would be a bounder,
    A cad, in fact, whom the best people shun ;
    "And so, old boy," says this fantastic Hun,
"The thing to do is stop this tiresome fight.
    Only a cad goes on until it's won.
Make peace and, take my word, I know what's right."
And blathering onward thus, he fades into the night.

17   *April 8*

The buds of beech are red, but not yet broken :
    At sunset they are like a ruby-mine.
The currant's little flowers have awoken,
    Pale green with purple edges ; and a line
    Of gooseberry-bushes' larger flowers shine.
Now blooms, in weedy plots that none unravels,
    Groundsel. A curlew utters eight or nine
Clear calls repeated, not as when he travels,
Lonely, to inland lakes from the sea's sands and gravels.

18

For then he calls but once over each hill,
    A solitary voice that thrills the air :
Now, in the season of the daffodil,
    He rests from wandering, near rushes where
    His mate is nesting, while from here and there
The pigeons tell the woods that it is Spring.
    Chaffinches in the apple-trees, all fair
With deep-pink buds, are gaily chirruping.
And would my rhymes came near to Earth as those they sing.

19   *April 9*

After clear stars last night a white mist rolled
    Above our windows, and then trailed away
All silver through the fields, past the bright gold
    Of poplars, in whose leaves the sunlight lay.
    And now the dandelions light the day,
As though they did the work of tiny suns;
    And the first pansy spreads her raiment gay ;
And garden daisies glow, the crimson ones.
And all these things are saved by far and unknown guns.

20

The white narcissi with their flaming centres
    Shine, and the bloom is still upon the pear ;
And every blossom that the wild bee enters
    Flashes back sunlight, brightening the air.
    A foreign apple-blossom glitters, fair
Under dark beech, and herons' eggs are broken,
    Their blue shells shining in the sunlight's glare
On moss and fern below the larch, in token
That the young brood above to daylight has awoken.

21

Now, where the branch-tips are like jewelled fingers,
    The spruce-trees brighten with a golden green ;
And later, day by day, the twilight lingers,
    Not only from the longer days, but sheen
    Of bright new leafage, as though Earth had been
Holding the sunlight longer with bright hands
    Which clutch the last glow of that hour serene
When the sun passes into distant lands
Waking the coloured birds that sing on alien strands.

22

One of the loveliest of butterflies,
    The orange-tip, is dancing on a ray
Of sunlight, and beside it there arise
    A couple of large-garden-whites that play
    About it as it glides upon its way
Beside green rambling tendrils to which roses
    Will come in June. And we have heard to-day
Koenigsberg falls ; and Death's great workshop closes,
Where Essen's wheels lie still, as though Bellona dozes.

        April 10

Bellona sleeps in these days! Can it be ?
    Not in the daylight in the open air,
Not in the shrinking lands of Germany ;
    Only where she keeps house with Death, and where
    She sits beside the factory fire, whose glare
Reddens the sky, at first by its own light,
    And, after, with the glow of towns that flare
In their last hours, and she loves that sight.
But drowsy now she sits in dark and silent night.

And not a wheel goes round, and not a fire
    Is lit, and no one opens now her door,
Where thousands used to work at her desire.
    Vainly she listens for the engines' roar.
    And Death is up and out upon the moor
Of Lüneberg. And cold and desolate
    Their house is now. Like gods that none adore
They soon will be, she and her grisly mate,
Seeing their temple void and no more consecrate.

25

And he will do his work in field and lane
    And city, even as he did of old,
But no more with the splendour she in vain
    Will yearn for when she wanders in the cold
    Of the world's disregard, her great house sold,
And no more incense of a flaming city.
    She will sit sorrowfully on the mould,
Waiting for better times, and more's the pity,
And singing, while she waits, some old and martial ditty.

26

The hyacinths are out below the trees,
    Where the gold daffodils have abdicated ;
And rocket, wandering on any breeze,
    Comes to small gardens, or has emigrated
    From ordered places, hedged and cultivated,
Into the woods to live among wild flowers,
    And has for some days now luxuriated.
Now the red-admiral sails across bright bowers,
And argus butterflies are seen in sunny hours.

27   *April* 11

The pear-tree snows its blossom to the ground,
    And cherry-blossom now is nearly over,
And no more bloom upon the plum is found.
    Through miles of perfect green goes now the drover
    Down Irish roads, and his free fellow-rover,
The tramp, who works for no man. Now are seen
    Small buds upon the lilac growing mauver.
Forsythia has lost its gold for green,
And kerria shines where that brighter gold has been.

Bright as the sun from which its colour came
    A berberis's bloom against the sky
Makes a wide flash as of an orange flame.
      And now a guelder-rose's opened eye
      Peers at Spring's pageantry, where hurries by
The bee upon his business, while there dances
    With lazy grace the brilliant butterfly
Upon a ray of sunlight, that enhances
The beauty of the world seen by his wandering glances.

29

And little leaves on oaks are just appearing,
    And all the buds upon the beech-trees fatten.
And ether throbs with great decisions nearing,
      And Mars on German fields begins to batten,
      And German cities that his engines flatten,
At last after so long. And Brunswick's falling,
    And into Magdeburg goes General Patton.
And Liberty is to her children calling
Bringing them home at last. And hushed is Hitler's brawling.

30   *April* 13

The fallen blossoms of the sycamore
    Drift one by one upon a stream all day,
Making their quiet journey, past a score
      Of bridges, past the murmur and the sway
      Of myriad branches, where the small flies play
In spirals and the trout leap up at them,
    Past fields where cattle graze and fields for hay,
At last to the broad river, with its hem
Of rushes, and the hills that are its diadem.

31

A dryad, nude and needing a fine dress
    From fairy tailors, or the fairy Queen
Herself, to be arrayed in gorgeousness,
      Might hold a silken scrap of brilliant green,
      Or lay it on her wrist to be well seen ;
So does the beech-tree at a branch's end
    Show a small patch of verdure that has been
Only one morning where the small twigs bend,
Waiting for what the golden days of Spring will send.

32

And now we mourn for Roosevelt, who when we
    And Liberty were weak and all alone
Came to our help, and stayed with us till he
    Could stay no more on Earth, whose tribes will own
    For long their debt to that great spirit flown,
And passing Victory upon her way
    To come into the fields whence he has gone.
And, but for her great haste, she would delay
To bless him, but sweeps on, nor would he have her stay.

33

Now apple-trees are shining pink and green,
    And with the wind leaves twinkle on the pear,
And over polyanthus may be seen
    A blow-fly resting still upon the air ;
    And an oak draws its gold cloak here and there
Over its mighty limbs, and the red glow
    Increases on the beech, which still is bare.
And monkshood has peeped out, and jonquils grow
And large anemones their alien splendour show.

34   *April* 14

Last night a young moon went into the West
    Through an old beech-tree, and its horns showed clear
Past the thin twigs, whose leaves are all at rest,
    Sleeping in buds, as sleeps an oak tree near
    And all the ash, though little leaves appear
On Spanish chestnuts, that like dreamers waking,
    With sunlight on their lashes, see and hear
Wide on the world's shore golden morning breaking.
And Tyranny upon his iron throne is quaking.

35   *April* 15

Ten months have gone since I began this lay
    Of the world's journey among leaves and flowers;
And standing, as a poet sometimes may,
    Outside our pastures and beyond our hours,
    I see a shape that in the distance lours
And rushes nearer, lit by far explosion
    And troubled by the rage of mighty powers.
It is the world, with all its land and ocean,
Returning to that point whence first I watched its motion.

And now bird-cherry blooms and scents the air,
    And leaves appear on boles of elm-trees low,
Though all the upper branches still are bare,
    But for the seed-pods, whose pale-golden glow
    Adds brightness to the day.   And now there go
Butterflies through the garden more and more,
    And the red peacock's eyes of azure show
Where he is floating down a path before
The early buds of thyme, until his dark wings soar.

37

Redder the beech to-day, the oak more gold,
    And brilliant on the larch its vernal sheen ;
Brighter the sycamore than can be told,
    And apple trees are now more pink than green,
    And on the chestnut its first blooms are seen.
And like to magic gold that fairies hide,
    But not completely, where the branches lean
Down from laburnums there may be descried
The gold of the bright buds, but not yet open wide.

Green leaves appear in an old beech's bole
    Ten feet above the ground, but not its own ;
An elder on a visit in a hole
    Among great branches has shot roots and grown,
    And shows the green the beech has not yet known.
White sunlight dazzles on the wings of rooks.
    And now the whitebeam's leaf is fully blown
And green buds hint of bloom.   A rock-rose looks
With blushes here and there out of a garden's nooks.

39

Not yet the swallows circle near our eaves,
    Though some have seen one, and the people say
That first they come to Tara.   Who believes
    The olden stories doubtless knows some lay
    Or legend telling by what hidden way
They fly to Ireland, and what ancient power
    Guides them across the spaces where they stray
Alone between the rainbow and the shower,
Leading them to their homes at the appointed hour.

And now I see them in the evening air,
    Wheeling above farm-buildings they have known,
. Under a pale-blue moon, lit by the glare
    Of sunlight, upward in the clear air thrown
    From under trees ! And now I hear the tone
Of their shrill cries, as old remembered things,
    After the thousand miles that they have flown,
Appear again below their gilded wings,
And round and round they go in swift rejoicing rings.

41 April 18

A chaffinch gathers dandelion clocks
    And slips away with them to line her nest
Over a garden wall, built of old blocks
    Of limestone on which dandelions rest ;
    And an elm sapling grows upon its crest
With bright leaves, though the older elms have none,
    And grass and ivy grow there with a zest,
Getting a gold light from the evening sun
Which touches their high wall when garden paths grow dun.

42

A rhododendron in its splendour glows,
    And speedwell, bluer than an Indian sky,
Shelters beneath, and the white guelder-rose
    Has opened, and a lilac wakes near by ;
    No lovelier flower hears the blackbird's cry
Thrilling the morning, and the golden stream
    Of a laburnum glitters like some high
Rock-nurtured cataract lit by earliest gleams
Of dawn while all the pools below are dark with dreams.

43

Now bugles, like a band of fairy men
    Marching together small and straight and blue,
Gleam where the beech are gathered in a glen
    With cypress, laurel, sycamore and yew,
    And one of speedwell's small relations too
Peeps from the grass. And now begin to shine
    The splendid candelabras white and new
Upon the chestnuts. And, where old leaves twine
About its oak-like leaves, shines the Great celandine.

44

The sun is red on beech and gold on swallows,
    As it drops westward. Now a jackdaw seems
Surprised at the new immigrants, and follows
    And dips to where they flash in the late beams,
    As though they had disturbed some curious dreams
He may have got from men, of isolation,
    Some local politics by which he deems
That he and his alone make up a nation.
But soon he wheels, to seek some saner occupation.

45   *April* 19

Now shines on the acacia the young green,
    And fuller the laburnum's golden flow.
Now circling pairs of butterflies are seen,
    And all the small birds sing and pheasants crow,
    And nimbly along boughs the squirrels go.
Bright are the hyacinths in shade of trees,
    And fair in all their haunts the cowslips blow,
And still the primroses in galaxies
Illuminate the wood, and mild is every breeze.

46

The tracks of snails are flashing in the sun,
    And overnight the daffodils have died :
Where there were thousands there is scarcely one.
    And suddenly to wakened woods has cried
    The cuckoo, coming from his wandering wide,
We know not where, to bring his voice again
    Into our ways, the two rich notes that glide
More hauntingly for what his fancies gain
From his strange wanderings in Africa or Spain.

47

Some beeches, like young men with fancy ties
    Or gaudy waistcoats, are decked out to-day
With all the splendour of Spring's draperies,
    The early green on which the sunbeams play
    Rejoicingly ; but older beeches stay
Still unadorned, except for the light dress
    That lichen gives their great limbs, grave and grey
Against the brilliance and the loveliness
Of flower and leaf and all the flash of Spring's excess.

48

And still the cuckoo calls, to find another,
      Or just to tell his native hills and vales
He has rejoined them and his foster mother.
      And, like an old friend that a traveller hails,
      The buttercup appears, with golden sails
Filled by mild winds. And London pride is glowing
      From small fat leaves, where an old dun avails
To give it shelter from the harsh winds blowing
Out of the North and East, and grey sand helps its growing.

49

Now the last blossom withers on the cherry
      And April loses one more lovely light.
We hear the sound of song from Canterbury
      Dropping from ether, and the self-same night
      We hear the tale of prisoners' dreadful plight
In Belsen ; as though Heaven rang its bells
      And Earth heard and at the same time had sight
Of open doorways of enormous hells
More near and dread and dark than any warning tells.

50   April 20

Into the house a bluebottle has flown
      Singing of Summer ; swallows find again
The fields they knew, fields their forbears have known
      Since ever they were fields : as though some lane
      Were in the air, some path that it were vain
For us to estimate, some airy hollow
      Worn by past wings, these wanderers from Spain
Follow the very curves they used to follow,
Knowing their twists and turns by some lore of the swallow.

51

Now, the first day since daffodils were over,
      In grass where plantain raises his dark head,
To flower comes one bud of the red clover,
      And mouse-ear chickweed's starry petals shed
      Their humble light. And now the white and red
Of chestnut-blossoms glow upon a stream
      And beech-husks drift there in a brown sheet spread,
And sometimes a laburnum's blossoms gleam,
And alder's bloom goes by, all as in some slow dream.

147

52

On strawberries wild and tame the blossom glows,
    And columbine's fair flowers in gardens wake.
And now another oak its foliage shows,
    And even the oldest of them starts to break
    In golden buds ; and the last petals shake
Down from the fruit-trees on a garden wall,
    But not the apple-blossoms, which still make
A glory in the orchards. And the call
Of blackbirds in the dawn is growing magical.

53

And now a foreign heath is all in bloom ;
    And yellow poppies, run a little way
Out of a garden, shine under the gloom
    Of cypresses ; and one white flower of may
    Wakes by the roadside, but the buds delay
To open yet, in April and so early,
    Although their myriads twinkle in the day,
Strung on the brilliant hedgerows pale and pearly
Under a warm blue sky and slow clouds white and curly.

54   *April* 21

Narcissus now succeeds the daffodil,
    And periwinkles peep from many a shade ;
And all the primroses are blooming still,
    And hyacinths are blue in every glade,
    And in their glory chestnuts are arrayed ;
And ants begin to march from cracks in walls
    And crevices in which their homes are made.
And Ireland listens to the blackbird's calls
While the world waits all hushed to hear when Berlin falls.

55   *April* 22

Now on the thorn the buds are like closed eyes
    That any light at any hour may waken,
But still among the leaves that round them rise
    They sleep, as in green seas sleeps on the kraken.
    Now yellow seed-pods from the elm-trees shaken
Drift with the chestnut-blossom on the stream,
    Which a slow way so long through vales has taken
That all we build or plant by it must seem
Shapes that its sleepy flow has fancied in a dream.

56

Mellow upon the trees falls evening.
    A fox steals out as softly as a star.
Birds in the beeches their late carols sing.
    And all the Irish fields are without scar,
    Saved by the men that fight for us afar.
It is to them we owe each leafy tree,
    Our young crops growing, green and safe from war,
And life, and more. And let us grateful be,
Or never after speak the name of Liberty.

57   *April 23*

Another rhododendron is in bloom
    And on its crimson flowers shines the green
Of a bright beetle : even in the gloom
    Of shadow it is bright, but than its sheen
    In sunlight nothing brighter can be seen
But emeralds, that from the dark of earth
    Gain light which insects from the sunshine glean.
This flower brought through half the planet's girth
Gives to our darker shrubs a splendour and a mirth.

58

Wild duck are hatching, and the she-duck plays
    The old game of the partly crippled wing,
And flutters off to lure whatever strays
    Too near her brood. The may is opening
    On branches that old trees are sheltering
On one side, while they see the sun go by
    All day upon the other, till there sing
The blackbirds all together, and there fly
The herons slowly home across a beryl sky.

59   *April 24*

And now the guelder-rose is blooming white,
    And round our garden all the shrubs are waking,
And whitebeams' blossoms open to the light,
    And the laburnum's cataracts are breaking,
    Broad now as though the dawn itself were taking
Its flashing way with water from the steep
    Of some wild mountain, where the fall was shaking
Thousands of golden nuggets from their sleep,
Water and dawn and gold in one tremendous sweep.

60

And Spring triumphantly pursues her way
    Northward, arrayed in gold and white and green,
And she is greeted from the air to-day
    By the Sixth Symphony, that work serene
    Beethoven made out of things heard and seen
In Springtime by a stream. We are as one
    Who meets by chance a spirit, and between
The two they share a house. So is begun
A partnership with us, whose course is guessed by none.

61

The mighty spirit dwelling in our homes
    Is wireless. Not in the Arabian Nights
Is any greater wonder. All that roams
    The ether he calls down from starry heights ;
    Music and words he brings, and even sights,
And instantaneous news from the world's end.
    What will he make of us ? What further flights
Of his wild fancy will what wonders send ?
And will good come or ill from our new magic friend ?

62
April 25

Now green leaves, with the seed-pods intertwining,
    Have dulled the brilliance of the elm-trees' gold,
And half the woods of beech like brass are shining,
    And half with ruddy buds, that barely hold
    The leaf, are glowing, and the oaks unfold
Their brilliant raiment. Now a small dark fly
    In silver circles more than may be told
Goes round above a stream. Like bits of sky
Fallen among the woods, the bright blue hyacinths lie.

63
April 26

A light rain falls and all the sky is grey,
    But in the oak-trees there is still a glow,
As though they gripped the light and made it stay
    Among their clutching twigs. Like melting snow
    The gleaming flowers on the chestnut blow,
And redder glow the buds that have not broken
    Upon the beech, and, where its young leaves show,
Earth seems to have in her own fields a token
Of all the noons and dawns that have in heaven awoken.

64

The dandelions overnight have set
  And what were like to suns are now like stars,
Galaxies gleaming faintly in the wet
  Green grass ; and where a pergola's thin spars
  Are rustically made of wooden bars
A purple clematis more richly gleams
  Than rarest silks of Africa's bazaars.
And on a mountain-ash the blossom seems
Just to be waking up from cool and snowy dreams.

65   *April 27*

Now through the ruddy buds of the last beeches
  To clothe themselves for summer, the green twinkles ;
And green and small under their glass are peaches ;
  And the acacia-leaves unfold their wrinkles,
  Whose old dull gold a passing shower sprinkles,
And brightens as it passes.   On the holly
  The white bloom sparkles ; and the periwinkles
Shine on in mossy places with a jolly
Smile on our neutral land, that cheers us in our folly.

66

Now like a ghost of Winter in the tomb
  Trailing its grey skirts in the haunts of Spring
A fall of hail has brought a minute's gloom
  To the bright land, which soon is glistening
  In sun again, till a storm wandering
Out of the North darkens the sky once more,
  And sunlight from its edges seems to fling
A glory at an oak, a sycamore,
And then a beech, and then leaves all dark as before.

67

Dittmar surrenders, Marshal Goering falls
  And from the fortress plaster drops away.
Now the façade from the great outer walls
  Comes crashing, and the odour of decay
  Reeks from the huge cracks that the light of day
Pours into, whence come voices as of bats,
  Troubling the ether, which complaining say
The Russians gather from the Asian flats,
Disturbing these sad things in their dark habitats.

Now may begins to gleam, like the first snow,
　In patches upon high rocks grey and bare,
That Winter brings the mountains while below
　Autumn is shining and September's air
　Is sunny still ; and the pink may is fair
With buds whose first deep blush is not yet seen.
　And brown are buds upon the ilex where
Its old limbs raise their fingers of dark green
For ever to the sun, all bright with their own sheen.

69

Still darker grows the fate of tyranny,
　A warning to the ages, one that they
Will never heed, for all through history
　Man and his masters go the same old way.
　His masters are those passions of a day
Forgotten, but still strong to hold his heart ;
　And all our laws, which single men obey,
Hold back a nation, once its armies start,
No more than hills may hold the sun that would depart.

70

An oak-tree shone with an unearthly light
　And like great clutching fingers came the hail,
And a whole rainbow glittered into sight ;
　And the storm passed into another vale,
　And there is blue sky through which pigeons sail ;
And like a scene too gaudy to be true,
　To show upon the stage some fairy-tale,
The beech and chestnut shine under the blue,
Where streaming from the West the golden rays come through.

71

Softly the German call's melodious notes
　Ring like a sheep-bell that a wolf might wear
About his neck at night, a wolf that gloats
　To wind his chosen prey in the night air,
　Though nearing his own end, but, unaware
Of what pursues him, tinkling still his bell.
　Then comes the voice, whose sneering tones lay bare
All that the bell would hide, cold tones that tell
News of the vast design to make the world a hell.

Now, as an orchestra tunes instruments
    For the last act of Götterdämmerung,
There come vague hints of varying events,
    And rumours reach us out of ether flung,
    False, true, in one aërial necklace strung,
All telling that the great and evil powers,
    That for so long have tortured, gassed and hung,
Are, with their blazing towns, in their last hours
And soon will go the way of April's stormy showers.

73

And flowers that now bud will bloom more fair
    For the departing of those shapes of evil
Going with smoke of ruin through the air,
    Like sulphurous clouds from some infernal revel
    Drifting away, forgotten by the Devil.
And comfrey, with its leaves like fairies' wings
    Still open while alighting on the level,
Will swing its mauve bells where the blackbird sings,
And peonies will bloom and all such lovely things.

74

What times we live in, who have walked with Mars !
    Mars has gone shopping in the London streets.
He has run suddenly across the stars
    To visit little houses ; now one meets
    That mighty figure daily, and he greets
Men, women, children in familiar way.
    It is as though great spirits left their seats
Upon Olympus and had come to stray
Along our garden paths, appearing in our day.

75

Well, Mussolini, you have had your fling.
    Perhaps the harm you did that has most weight
Is—you taught Hitler how to be a king.
    You helped to save the world in '38,
    But not for long. And now you meet your fate.
And we have no rejoicings at your fall.
    Strange what a preference the Roman state
Had ever for such men, and how they all,
Or nearly, went your way to sudden funeral.

76

Pardon me, Clio, that my pen should tell
    Of things like these, which meant to tell of flowers;
But as we listen to the passing-bell
    Of mighty tyrannies in iron towers
    It turns my thoughts awhile from vernal hours
And from the happy birds that have no plan
    But to make musical the April showers,
And through the night of Time I turn to scan
The dark and desperate way trod by the feet of Man.

            77

The little waxen bells of the arbutus
    Swing now, and thyme is out and geum too;
And Hitler sinks, whose airmen tried to shoot us
    Coming from Greece. But let that pass. The blue
    Of monkshood shows, and from dark leaves peeps through
Cotoneaster's little starry bloom,
    And what was brown turns greener on the yew,
And gold and crimson shines a brilliant broom,
And ether throbs with hope, and Earth prepares a tomb.

            78

The peacock butterflies on tulips settle
    And a sweet-scented iris is all gold,
And by a pig-sty blooms the red dead-nettle,
    And dark-blue lupins from their buds unfold,
    Though winds are from the North and blowing cold.
And starrily a small white clematis
    Gleams on a pergola, whose bars uphold
Roses and honeysuckle, which the kiss
Of April will not wake, nor all May's ecstasies.

            79   *April* 30

The sunlight glitters in the copper-beech;
    A frost leaps out at night, attacking Spring;
Skirts of retreating Winter seem to reach
    Across the sky, dark grey and menacing
    All ragged at the edges, as might cling
A tattered cloak to one that lurks and prowls
    Along a frontier where he once was king
And now is exiled, lonely among owls,
But hoping to return, where a far watch-dog howls.

80

The heavy heads of poppies, not yet bloomed,
  Droop, and the budding lupins, with the blow
That Winter struck them, though they thought him doomed ;
  And the potatoes are all lying low,
  And early blossoms now will never grow
To strawberries, and here and there the head
  Of a proud tulip bends, and green leaves show
That the chrysanthemums are hurt or dead,
And apples may escape and yet be harvested.

81

A hail-storm passes white across the land
  Between us and the splendour of the trees,
Like a thin curtain by an unseen hand
  Drawn, or like ghosts that ride upon a breeze.
  It passes, and in brilliant sun one sees
The golden oak, the beech, and, flashing plain,
  The chestnuts' blooms in starry galaxies,
And young leaves of that traveller from Spain,
The other chestnut ; and the poplars glow again.

MAY

A bright May morning and a night of frost,
   And in the morning air a certain glow.
Is't only from the sun, whose light is tossed
   Abundantly this morning to and fro,
   From little clouds that past it racing go,
On to our oaks and beeches ? Or does light
   From no material source portend the woe
Of peoples ending ? Is the awful night
Lifting from Europe's fields ? Is Victory in sight ?

Indeed the glow by which our oaks were brightened
   Was interwoven with a light enchanted ;
One lit our eyes, the other our hearts lightened ;
   For news came that the spirit which has haunted
   And darkened Europe, and which nearly daunted
Liberty's self, has left the world it troubled,
   Passing from Berlin, where it long had vaunted,
Along whose streets the blood now ran and bubbled
Because of his mad dream. And mankind's hope is doubled.

3

What can one say of such a monstrous wretch ?
   Let history say it. Buttercups appear
In greater numbers, and a dark blue vetch
   Blooms in the garden. Many leaves are sere
   And blossoms nipped. Too early in the year
Spring came among us, and this backward stroke
   Of Winter at the flowers strikes us here
Like a sword drawn from under a dark cloak.
But still the beech shine on, and golden is the oak.

4

Jimmy McCloskey died, we hear to-day,
    Of wounds received in action, and though Fame
Has never known him, yet my rustic lay
    Is more adorned by this young soldier's name
    Than by the names of those that have brought shame
On Europe and mankind, and whose mad rages,
    Whose cold designs and predatory aim,
Have brought the shadow of the old dark ages
Close to our door and day, and blackened history's pages.

5

Now Wietinghoff, that German salamander,
    With all of his nine hundred thousand men,
Surrenders to Sir Harold Alexander.
    So ends the story that at Alamein
    Had its beginning in the desert, then
Two thousand miles of cape and promontory
    Mountain and isle and vineyard, hill and fen,
Saw written for the ages this great story
Which shone at noon to-day with its completed glory.

Now falls Berlin, the den of that wild beast
    Whose pile of skulls surpasses Tamerlane's
As the Great Pyramid o'ertops the least
    Of pyramids that are on Egypt's plains ;
    And brief must be the period that remains
For his wild dream to ravage Europe more,
    Which among all the curses and the banes
Left by ill spirits flitting from Earth's shore
Is still the darkest load lying at mankind's door.

7

May 3

And there were callers, so we hear to-day,
    At Germany's legation over here
To express sorrow in respectful way
    And possibly to drop a quiet tear,
    Because the man who would have ruled the sphere,
Enslaving everyone that should be willing
    To be a slave, has ended his career
Of torture, plunder, tyranny and killing,
And, though blood flows, no more for him (alas !) is spilling.

8

But, what concerns me more, flowers and leaves
     In thousands by the last few frosts are slain.
Ev'n the forget-me-not in gardens grieves,
     As if a blow that she could ill sustain
     Had fallen, though she comes of an old strain
Native to these isles, knowing all the ways
     And whimsies of our climate, which again
Hurls through the atmosphere that should be May's
The sleet and hail and ice of January's days.

9

I think the dandelions' clocks will last
     Longer than the third Reich of Germany,
Though they are white and full and any blast
     Of wind may waft them through the greenery,
     Where every seed will sink and dreamily
Lie in the earth through winter till the year
     Brings April round again, and we shall see
Once more their blaze of tiny suns appear
As strange beasts see the sun in planets far from here.

10   *May* 4

An old beech is not yet in green arrayed
     Among the rest, but, like a young man singing
Snatches of song, it flashes in the shade
     Of its dark limbs a front of leafage springing
     On small twigs here and there, though birds are winging
And warbling in warm air and it is time
     That even the oldest beech should give up clinging
To the old ways of Winter, though his clime
Steals back at nights to strew the leaves and grass with rime.

11

Now grandly the first peony appears,
     And more and more the may shines out like snow
Fallen upon green branches, and one hears
     One symphony from birds all round, as though
     Somewhere unseen, in trees' shade or below
A rhododendron's glory, Pan himself
     Conducted that strange music all birds know,
Or deputizing, on some weedy shelf
Of an old rockery, flower-hid, stood an elf.

12

And upon upper branches in the sun
  The pink may now is in its opening hour,
And, as a cardinal outshines a nun,
  So it outshines the white may's humbler flower.
  And yet in that plain bloom there is a power
To call back years from very far away
  And, though the frown of Time between us glower,
I see the radiance of an earlier May,
Whence scarce a prophet guessed the thunder of to-day.

13

A butterfly alights upon the lip
  Of a blue porcelain frog. It seems indeed
That all the triumphs of our workmanship
  Are only for Man's eye : no other breed
  Heeds them a moment, or will only heed
Our image as a rock on which to rest,
  Or on the curve of some proud statue's ear
A bird may choose a place to build its nest.
Our arts are nought to them, and theirs beyond our quest.

14

A fern-leaved beech puts out its graceful leaves
  Like fairy fingers. Let us never see
These lovely things, or, later, the ripe sheaves
  Of harvest, without thanks said silently
  To those who saved our fields and every tree,
By fighting far away, from such a doom
  As shadowed Poland, Denmark, Italy,
France, Norway, Belgium, Greece, and made a tomb
Of Holland, and now win, so that our flowers bloom.

15

Now appears mustard's wild and lovely gold
  With jade-green leaves, called sometimes the wild rape.
There's nothing more to wait for : men behold
  Only the crumbling of that fearful shape
  That threatened mankind, but its raiments drape
Decay and rust : the thing itself is dead.
  And whether the great sword, that we escape
So narrowly, falls to the left, instead
Of clattering to the right, has no need to be said.

159

L

16

The thing is over, and we lose a woe,
    And our own dangers close round us again,
Lurking more secretly than did the foe.
    Man to cheat man will once more work amain,
    And we, who cannot even grind our grain,
Must eat instead of bread whatever given
    And drink strange chemicals, till by some plain
And barbarous folk we shall again be driven
To fight for life, more weak than when we last had striven.

17

At eight o'clock we hear Holland is free
    And Denmark, and our prisoners of war,
Many a thousand, and at last they see
    The day they dreamed of and have waited for
    Through years so long.   Again the din and roar
Of one more limb from the colossus falling
    With bits of broken armour to the floor,
The dead colossus that is done with brawling.
And we've no need to choose twixt death and servile crawling.

18

What is this fearful figure that lies prone,
    But for a few limbs that still lean and sway
Against the framework of a mouldering throne
    Amongst a spreading odour of decay,
    Heavy with monstrous armour ?   Come away,
For there is deadly danger in it yet,
    And famine and diseases that obey
The dead colossus will sweep thence, a threat
To cities in all lands where mankind's homes are set.

19   *May 5*

The birds to-day are singing in the rain
    As though they cared that mankind's grief is ending ;
But less than we should care for any pain
    In other planets are the birds intending
    A sign of joy that at long last the rending
Of mankind's dwellings ceases ; for the swallow
    Is not among the singers, who suspending
Her nest from eaves, or building in some hollow
In old barns, may perchance glance at the way we follow.

20

The traitor voice from Hamburg sneers no more.
 Where go such voices when they drift from here?
In what hell do they echo? Or by shore
 Of Lethe do they gather, with each sneer
 That ever issued from a false lip's leer?
There with old lies among weeds foul and rotten
 To fester into silence, where ghosts hear
Only slow waves, and all things are forgotten;
While he that uttered them flees North towards Lofoten.

21

The rain sweeps hence, and all the gravel shines.
 Only among the trees a shower falls
From leaf to leaf; a far wood glows like mines
 Of fairy gold appearing on the walls
 Of some sheer cliff; and now a pigeon calls,
And blackbirds beyond number seem to say
 That Spring is back, and hold their festivals,
While Winter's last grim rearguard prowls away
And beams are streaming bright into the golden day.

22

Now all the moss is brighter for the rain,
 And dandelions' round white heads are bare,
Though still a few of their white clocks remain,
 No greater in proportion than the share
 The Germans hold of what their fortunes were
Before they followed (as a man at night
 Follows a shape of phosphorus and air
Over a deep marsh to a dreadful plight)
The lure of Hitler, till they lost his fatal light.

23

And shieldferns make a brightness in the woods,
 And hartstongue flourishes, and on the trees
Lichen is greener, and the lilac's buds
 Have opened in their glory, and one sees
 The blue seeds shining on the cypresses,
Whose scented boughs are alien to our isle
 And strange to us. And still the bumblebees
Have the blue hyacinths, which strangely smile
In the red level rays at evening for a while.

24

A Himalayan poppy's lovely head
   Is shining bluer than an Indian sky,
If anything is bluer. Now half dead
    Are the laburnum's blooms, which should not die
    Till May is over and midsummer nigh.
But Winter's last hard stroke has seared their edges.
    A mountain-ash blooms, and the buds near by
Are white on an acacia, and the hedges
Are fair with may, and streams now cloak themselves with sedges.

25

And now the corncrake calls to us again,
    Whose flight across a single field will go
Or cross a continent, from here to Spain.
    About the feet of an old oak tree grow,
    Rooted in moss, the ferns that gardeners know
As polypody. Leaves of many trees
    Are smitten by the frost, and all the glow
Of rhododendrons fades, although one sees
Spring triumphing again, and nights no longer freeze.

26   *May* 7

Now pink buds on cotoneasters turn
    To white blooms here and there, and on wild walls
With nothing trained upon them, a small fern
    Called spleenwort grows, and all around it crawls
    Ivyleaf-toadflax, whose mauve flower sprawls
Over untended places ; and now whitens
    The shrub called snow-in-summer ; and rain falls
And sets the blackbirds singing, and then lightens,
And the gold sun appears and all the valley brightens.

27

The lovely palaces of Prague are free,
    Where once, when Masaryk was President,
I knew the kindly hospitality
Of Czechs' and Slovaks' rightful Government,
    And we rejoice that Freedom's banishment
From that fair land will end in a few hours
    And that the last oppressors will be sent
Back to the ruins of their martial towers
And Spring will find all free in her Bohemian bowers.

28

The beechmast on a stream lies thick and brown
   And slowly drifts till, coming to a weir,
It quickens slightly, and then hurries down,
   And rapider becomes the stream's career.
   And here a chestnut-blossom sails, and here
Dark bits of moss, and a bright bloom of may,
   Or, like a gold ship with an elf to steer,
Goes a laburnum's bloom upon its way
Across the shade of trees and golden light of day.

29

The blackbirds' chorus in the early morning,
   Singing to greet the sun's first flood of gold,
Gave the last dreams of night some hint, some warning,
   That there were glorious tidings to be told.
   For mighty spirits such as Victory hold
Converse with simpler things than such as we.
   At eight we hear Bellona's car is rolled
Back to Valhalla's hells, whence so long she
Has driven through the world at hest of Germany.

30   *May* 8

This is the day that we have waited for !
   This is the day we have foreseen so long,
When only faith foresaw it and no more.
   This is the day that, when the foe was strong
   And we were weak and must endure his wrong,
We felt would rise up some time with the sun.
   No more the sirens ; now the blackbirds' song.
May we be worthy of the victory won.
If not, how many ghosts will deem their work undone !

31

And they will haunt us at our cocktail bars.
   We must be something better than we were.
Wars do not come by chance from evil stars,
   Nor only because enemies prepare.
   They come where men are weak and unaware
When on a people's aims are specks of rust ;
   For spiritual things when lacking care
Can rust like steel, and, when they go, the dust
Covers material things more swiftly than it must.

32

This is a golden day, even to see,
Besides its glorious place in history's pages.
It is a day for butterfly and bee,
    Bright as it will appear to future ages,
    This day on which the six-years war assuages.
The Star-of-Bethlehem comes out to-day
    Low in the grass ; and hushed are Hitler's rages,
And all the storms they raised have rolled away,
And there is thankfulness, that words are weak to say.

33

The oldest beech's leaves to-day are shining
    Which came last night, with Peace ; and crowned with gold
Are silver leaves upon the grass reclining ;
    And over meadows as the day grows old
    A heron goes to where his wings will fold,
Lazily, lazily, as though the woe
    Of myriads were nothing, and he told
With every beat of his wide wings and slow
He knows of our just Cause no more than neutrals know.

34

And now through ether we can hear the voices
    From London and from hamlets in the shires
With which a people, troubled long, rejoices,
    And bells are ringing in Parisian spires,
    While in our sky there roam the wandering fires
Of lightning, as though Thor in surly mood
    Grumbles that there are no more funeral pyres,
And the Valkyries slay not as he would,
And Prussia's bad old gods all thirst for lack of blood.

35   *May 9*

Yes, bad old gods had part in Prussia's war,
    For Hitler's mind, inflamed by ancient stories,
Acted as Odin would have done, or Thor,
    Or any awful figure to whom gore is
    A soothing drink and flaming towns are glories.
Now sink the flames, and bad gods disappear
    With Hitler's dreams and ancient allegories,
Till sloth or sleep of ours shall lure them here
To riot once again upon their fell career.

36

Grey in the shade and silver in the sun
   Small flies are circling swiftly where a stream
Carries down blossoms whose career is done
     And a brown sheet of beechmast, where there gleam
     Laburnum-blossoms still, and old trees dream
Above it of the lands from which they came ;
     For trees can travel now from the extreme
Of the world's distance. Still, as with a flame
The ether throbs and thrills, and echoes Victory's name.

37   *May* 10

The gorgeous peony is in full bloom,
   And iris are beginning to appear,
Yellow, pale blue and purple ; but a gloom
     Is on the whitebeam's flowers, for the year
     Smiled brightly, but too early, and all sere
Are early leaves and blossoms. Now remain
     Few dandelions' clocks. The lupins rear
Their blue and purple spires. Where any lane
Is mown, the daisies shine. And lilac comes again.

38   *May* 11

Rock-roses form a single mass of red,
   And buttercups appear a sheet of gold.
Like strips of linen on the mown grass spread
     Are daisies. On a briar now unfold
     The petals of two roses, and behold
The sunlight earlier than they have done
     In other years. Protected from the cold
In their glass house begonias have won
To their full bloom, and birds are singing in the sun.

39

And still in ether ring the thanks of Earth
   For its deliverance, from many isles
And realms far inland, wherein joy and mirth
     Are seen where for five years there were no smiles
     And hunger marched, well drilled, a thousand miles.
That joy and mirth we see not here, but we
     See glory in the eyes of two exiles
Returning home, Justice and Liberty ;
For these and other shapes the eyes of poets see.

40

Now, lovelier than its name, weigelia blooms,
    And now dianthus and the small wood-sanicle.
And grasses have put on their summer plumes
    And the cow-parsnip spreads its flat white panicle,
    Unthreatened now by any force tyrannical,
Which would have shadowed all the fields we know
    With its cold might, relentless and mechanical.
But into darkness its red banners blow,
To be with dreadful things that happened long ago.

41 *May* 12

Last night a corncrake called the whole night long,
    Pausing to let the blackbirds greet the day
With all the wonder of their early song ;
    Deep in the field where I began my lay
    One day in June when they cut last year's hay.
Upon the field's north side we heard her call,
    Just where one used to call so long last May,
And fifty years ago, and during all
The ages that have known green grass there growing tall.

42

Dames-violet upon a roadside stands,
    Haply escaped from little gardens near,
Jumping the road and peering at green lands
    From the bank's top.   Herb-bennets now appear
    With little golden faces, and the year
Begins to bring the elder-flower again.
    Ash saplings are in leaf, but the severe
Grey limbs of older ash-trees still remain
Bare below shining boughs that crown the hill of Glane.

43 *May* 13

Dull now below their leaves are elm-trees pods,
    And now herb-robert from the roadside peeps,
And fallen, fallen are the German gods,
    So that no horror on our landscape leaps ;
    And some thank God to-day, while Ireland sleeps.
And some say, "Well, I'm glad the war is over.
    I think it's a good thing.   We shall have jeeps
Upon the road again.   Cattle and drover
Have had it long enough."   Still brighter grows the clover.

Now shine the rhododendrons in the woods,
    That treasure of the Himalayas' vales :
Few flowers of all Nature's inspired moods
    Are lovelier ; and now the bluebell pales
    And droops below the beeches. Now there sails
A crescent moon low in the evening sky.
    Out of their forest of thick grass the snails
Appear upon mown borders. Merrily
The primrose still looks up where the blue hyacinths die.

Now lilies-of-the-valley, which grow wild
    Among the wooded vales of Gloucestershire,
Swing their white bells to strong winds blowing mild,
    Sheltered by garden walls ; and now a spire
    Of sorrel rises, as though touched with fire,
From the deep grass. And blackbirds' songs are merry
    And all the trees are ringing with their quire,
Because they see the ripening of the berry
On plant and bush, and watch a glow light up the cherry.

Now the white blossom of the dogwood shows,
    And down the streams drift petals of the may.
And now the circles of grey flies that rose
    Above our stream are heavy clouds that sway
    From bank to bank ; below them drifts away
A heron's feather. Near it on her nest
    A woodcock among brown leaves that decay
With last year's foliage rests as brown stones rest,
Invisible as though with leaves and old twigs dressed.

The strong wind from the West goes southwards now.
    Buttercups look like strips of cloth-of-gold
Laid on the grass. Upon the ash-tree's bough
    Are tiny leaves that do not yet unfold,
    The last of all the leaves to risk the cold,
Which from our fields the veering wind has blown.
    Leaning upon a wall, the pear-trees hold
Small pears no thicker than a finger grown.
Pyrus japonica still flames against grey stone.

48

A Turkey-oak is last, except the ash,
    To wave its young green foliage to the Spring.
Twigs on the trunk of an old oak-tree flash
    Orange and red, though green is glimmering
    From all its branches. No more blossoms swing
Upon the chestnuts ; for the frost which came
    So late and bitterly, when birds should sing,
Has seared them and some leaves, as with a flame,
And there is widespread loss of blossoms wild and tame.

49

Horse-radish in the garden flowers white,
    And achillea, kin to humble yarrow ;
And under glass the golden bloom is bright,
    Whence Summer gives us vegetable-marrow.
    Rosemary blooms among green leaves and narrow,
All pale beneath. Chaffinch and bullfinch see
    The garden grow ; but the world-wandering sparrow
Is now away near cottages, where she
Builds in the thatch her nest more warm than in a tree.

50   *May* 17

Now the blooms open on an Austrian rose
    All withered. An acacia's leaves hang dead.
And all the blossoms of the whitebeam froze
    When the frost came in April ; and instead
    Of green leaves on the walnut there are spread
Brown bunches on the branches in decay.
    And now one dog-daisy has heralded
The coming of the Summer, far away
Although she be as yet, by shores of some blue bay.

51

For Summer now has touched the coast of Spain,
    Or in Algeria withers up the green,
Or sits in Egypt on the sandy plain
    And listens to the sighs of the khamseen,
    That whispers of the wastes where he has been,
Where water is illusion. On the ground
    In Cairo now is lying the serene
Blue of the jacaranda, as though round
The trunks there lay a strip of the sky's blue profound.

52

Now thyme is all a mass of little blooms
    And fills the air about it with the scent
That roams along the slopes the sun illumes
    All through the summer upon downs of Kent ;
    And geums that have bloomed since April went
Are at their best, some scarlet and some gold.
    And chives, although their destiny is meant
But for the kitchen, gaily now uphold
Their purple heads.   And blooms of cabbages unfold.

53

Some jackdaws that have shared a house with me
    Have hatched their young, whose voices we can hear
High in the ivy, and a neighbouring tree
    Hides more of them.   Man's neighbours they appear,
    For always they and we build somewhere near.
I hope they still approve of us, although
    The ways they knew are changing, and I fear
That if we separate we shall not go
By ways as smooth as those the jackdaws used to know.

54   *May* 18

Now roses bloom upon the garden wall
    And there are gleaming the white flowers of peas.
And now the lupins have grown strong and tall
    And glow like twilight upon southern seas,
    And all the raspberry bushes sing with bees.
And Star-of-Bethlehem is open wide
    (Where the deep grass runs in among the trees)
Striped green and white upon the under side,
And white above as stars that through the evening ride.

55

The water-wagtail's young grey-breasted brood
    Are out upon the mudbanks by a stream
That flows by lazily along a wood,
    Reflecting sunlit trees as in a dream
    A little brighter than the real trees seem.
The gorgeous petals of the peony
    Begin to fall and in a circle gleam.
And now cotoneaster merrily
Sparkles upon a wall with all its galaxy.

Now under glass one Canterbury bell,
    One single bloom, is showing ; and still shine
Many anemones, surviving well
    The April frost that lately thinned their line.
    A wind blows, but the day is warm and fine,
And small-brown-heaths are dancing now in pairs
    Their airy dances ; and the columbine
Is blooming with the lupins, and mauve tares
Glow in the wilder lands, which the small medick shares.

57

The crimson rhododendron that too soon
    Put forth its flowers, and so met the frost
Which came about the full of April's moon
    And withered blossoms through the garden tossed,
    Has now replaced the early blooms it lost
With flowers in their utmost splendour glowing.
    The tendrils of a purple vetch have crossed
A bunch of grasses in a meadow growing.
And pollen from the pines along the air is blowing.

58

Now hyacinths are dead, and nearly over
    Are cowslips, and the primroses are few,
And thicker grow the clusters of red clover,
    And some white clover lights the meadows too ;
    And tottie grass, that shakes the summer through,
Has just appeared, but is not fully spread.
    And the forget-me-nots, still turquoise blue,
Remember April, and a dark brown head
Nods on the woodrush now, and sorrel grows more red.

59

Now Victory has come to us as though
    She rode a barque on a tempestuous sea,
And storms, that brought her, still about her blow
    And shake the world that she has come to free.
    Too dark the future to guess what shall be.
Few lights by which to see when men shall rest.
    Famine is unsubdued ; and with him he
May rise who fears no conquerors, the Pest.
And who knows what may come to harm us from Trieste ?

A shrub with little leaves and little flowers,
    Smaller than lilies-of-the-valley, grows
Outside the garden, shining in the showers
    That fell last night, for on the leaf there glows
    A gloss as on the laurel.   Where none mows
The weeds it stands and gives a gentle stare,
    As though the nettles in their ragged rows
About it had no business to be there.
Pernethia its name, as alien as its air.

61

The rain inspired a host of birds to sing,
    And slugs come out from long grass on to mown ;
And bugles, now grown tall, are brightening
    The shade under the beech-trees ; and the drone
    Of pigeons fills the air, though not yet grown
To the full volume that all through July
    Gives to the warm air such a sleepy tone.
Now grey and full of clouds is all the sky,
And there the wind cries out as he goes racing by.

62

More than half full the moon, and that strange light
    We know as twilight now begins to glow
Between the borders of the day and night ;
    A more enchanted green the beech-trees show,
    And the green meadowlands, than when they were
Lit only by the sun ; and the pale dome
    Is like a magic crystal, through which go
Late swallows, and the flocks of rooks fly home
And all the wandering birds that through the evening roam.

63

The world has many glories, many wonders ;
    Sahara's desert and the Asian flowers,
Africa's lightnings and enormous thunders,
    Volcano, avalanche, and other powers ;
    But not a tropic has this light of ours,
That lingers on our lawns as the long day
    In Summer glides out of the glimmering bowers
That twilight blesses, and then steals away,
While, silver through pale blue, sparkles a planet's ray.

Above our garden wall where plum-trees grow,
    Cherries and pears, the one towards the West,
The little clocks of dandelions glow ;
    And sometimes seedling trees come there to rest,
    Hazel and elm, upon the pebbly crest ;
And toadflax grows there, and from the far side
    Cotoneaster climbs, now at its best,
And leans over the top ; and, rambling wide,
The ivy runs, and grass flows over like a tide.

65

And over it hydrangea lifts its head
    To peer into the garden, but the cold
Had withered it and all its flowers are dead.
    Outside a cypress lifts its tower of gold.
    And macrocarpa, a tree great and old,
Stands with its many buttresses, which all
    Join in one trunk, that rises to uphold
The dark green branches high above the wall,
Out of whose sombre shade the unseen blackbirds call.

66

And by the golden cypress stands a tree
    With branches drooping in a shower of light,
A weeping elm, whose green cascade you see
    Over the wall ; and to a greater height
    A Scotch fir rises ; and they have the sight,
From garden paths, of other cypresses,
    Green fountains spreading beside beech more bright,
And oaks that grow slow through the centuries.
And Wellingtonias lift over all of these.

67

And weeping beech and fernleaved beech are here,
    And cryptomeria japonica,
And variegated oaks, which every year
    Backward a little further seem to stray
    Towards the plain green leaves that now array
The other oaks ; and there a weeping ash
    Makes a wide tent, whose green sides lightly sway
As winds go by and passing showers splash.
And ragged-robins in the grass begin to flash.

68

And copper beech behind the green leaves glows,
　　And here and there a holly, and one lime ;
But the full list is suited more to prose,
　　Which holds more weight of fact than can a rhyme
　　Upon its journey through the wastes of Time,
Travelling light and carrying those things
　　That art from solid matter can sublime,
And which are not too heavy for the wings
Of Pegasus to bear in his far wanderings.

69

Now under glass there shines a starry flower
　　Called tradiscanthia, whose leaves are green
And purple, and which tumbles in a shower
　　Over the pot's edge ; and close by is seen
　　One flame-like bud that for some days has been
Increasing on a cactus ; and a few
　　Carnations' bright and perfumed faces lean
On their long stalks ; and now gleam one or two
Geraniums, which are of Summer's retinue.

70　　　　　　　　　　　　　　*May 22*

A white valerian comes out like a star ;
　　And in its glass house the strange cactus-bud
Has opened, like a camp-fire seen afar,
　　Glowing at night with logs of smouldering wood,
　　Which break in sudden flame ; as red as blood
With sunlight on it, the wide flower glows,
　　With twenty petals pouring out a flood
Of gorgeous colour, such as Asia knows,
And more akin to fire than ever is our rose.

71　　　　　　　　　　　　　　*May 23*

Now, like church bells by one another chiming,
　　A large white clematis's flowers sway.
Beside a wakened honeysuckle, climbing
　　Golden and odorous where bars display
　　The rambling blossoms that along them stray
Where darker clematis has bloomed and where
　　There has not come as yet the roses' day.
And still a few small clematis are there,
Like little galaxies beyond the great stars' glare.

72

Now the last buds upon the ash have broken,
    And bright the foliage that came so late.
The dogwood's small four-pointed stars have woken ;
    And, like the first red sparks to radiate
    From fires new-lit, within the garden gate
The red valerian begins to glow.
    Tall with their purple hoods, there congregate
The monkshoods in the garden, where there grow
Only the lupins now with a more splendid glow.

73

Though this is but a chronicle of flowers
    And trees and grasses and some butterflies,
And though on Europe still immensely lours
    Disastrous smoke, or only starts to rise ;
    Yet from that scene I turn away my eyes,
And from the rustic scenes that I have shown,
    To mourn the loss of one grown old and wise
So long, Napoleon's victor she had known
And lived to see the might of Hitler overthrown.

74

So Lady Jersey passes hence.   She saw,
    And was a part of, that stability
That England raised against the natural law
    Of Time and Change.   So strong it seemed to be,
    That buttress against Change, eternity
Seemed to be in its ramparts.   Yet she knew
    More change than came in all the pageantry
Of ages since the conquest.   Horses drew
Coaches when she was young, and her grandchildren flew.

And yet by any of these wonders no man
    Saw her surprised ; but like a mountaineer
Firm on a sliding surface, or a Roman
    Saying nil admirari in the ear
    Of any that should wonder, she would hear
The doctrines of so many changing days,
    And the new customs that the young hold dear,
So that her friends were spread through time and place,
People of many creeds and far divergent ways.

Many will miss her as a guide that stood
    Visible in the rushing of the ages
Not all submerged by their enormous flood,
    Standing till yesterday against their rages,
    And needing no memorial in these pages,
But living on in many memories,
    One to be numbered with the quiet sages
Whose serene lives and happy destinies
Brought calm among the storms of time and lands and seas.

77 *May 24*

Dark-blue veronica begins to bloom,
    And pinks are budding and the iris glow,
And bishopweed's bright galaxies illume
    Untended spaces, and the blossoms blow
    Pale-green upon the spindlewood and show
Their four small petals dimly, and there come
    Large butterflies rejoicing to a row
Of geums flashing sunlight, and from some
Goes up the bumblebee's prolonged and busy hum.

78 *May 25*

A rainy morning, and the swallows fly
    So low over a field which grows to hay
That more rain must be coming by and by.
    Himmler is dead, as we heard yesterday,
    And Hell has no Legation where men may
Express their grief, and Germany's Legation
    In Dublin is shut up. So who would say
How sad he is must make his lamentation
All by himself, till Hell sends legates to each nation.

79

Or have I overlooked the fact that Hell
    Sets up its embassies in every town,
With diplomatic privilege to sell
    Disease on which no law has dared to frown?
    To one of these bad houses should go down
Whoever would condole for Himmler's death.
    There let the tears fall till the spiders drown.
There let the words be said that Satan saith:
Heil Hitler! And again Heil Hitler with each breath.

175

M

Or haply in that counterfeiters' den
    Where herrings are dyed brown and pink and gold
With creosote, to cheat a world of men
    And spoil the hard work done in wet and cold
    And storm by fishermen, there is unrolled
The flag of Hell's Legation, mournfully
    Drooping for Himmler, who worked well of old
For Hell and Hitler against Liberty,
As these against mankind and against honesty.

81

Rain falls and, like the Canterbury bells,
    We stay indoors, for under glass they grow
And every hour or so a new bud swells.
    And the blue poppies in the garden show
    Their lovely petals, but this year are slow
To show them, as though haunted even yet
    By fear of frost, which dealt them such a blow
And in our orchard, ere the blossom set,
Killed every apple when died the last violet.

82

They buried Himmler in a grave unknown
    And unmarked. But, were monument to be
For such as him, there might be carved in stone
    The shapes of Violence and Cruelty,
    With Justice standing over them, and she
Armed, but as though she snatched a sword while sleeping,
    And only just in time, now terribly
Bringing the great blade downward, widely sweeping
To make an end at last, at last, to the world's weeping.

83

More rain to-day, and all the birds rejoice,
    As with one acclamation : every bush
Rings with the singing of its hidden voice
    In gardens where small pears begin to blush
    And blackbird, bullfinch, chaffinch, tit and thrush
See the pinks blossom and the lupins blaze,
    And tall white iris with an orange flush
Upon their lower lips, and wait the days
When all the fruit is ripe along the garden's ways.

84

Now London pride is like a pink sea-mist,
    Seen on the sky-line of a little mound.
Hedge-parsley flowers, growing where it list,
    With ferny leaves. And now show hard and round
    The heads of knapweed, whose roots underground
Run for at least a yard, wiry and shallow ;
    And the dark-headed plantains now abound ;
And here and there begins to bloom a mallow.
The first delphiniums wake, which June's long days will hallow.

85   *May 28*

Now elder-blossoms are by roadsides gleaming
    And honeysuckle is on cottage walls.
A storm along the Dublin mountains streaming
    Raged all this morning, but as evening falls
    They are as calm as ever. Never palls
Their huge serenity. Below are spread
    Upon their feet the flowery festivals
Of many gardens, where azaleas shed
Their blossoms on the lawns, and salvia lifts its head.

86

And sometimes in the sunlight bright and warm
    A tree would flash like a green meteor's glare
Against the sable splendour of the storm,
    Or some bright field of mustard shone as fair
    As elfin gold, more fine than gold is where
They mine it in known earth. Jerusalem sage
    Was shining yellow in the Dublin air,
And stocks were out, for Dublin is a stage
Ahead of gardens' growth in the Meath pasturage.

87   *May 29*

And now the first of the sweetwilliams peep
    From sheltered places, and the cranesbill shows
Its dark blue flower, and syringas sleep
    A little longer ; and one yellow rose
    Comes to the garden, earliest of those
That will give glory to the summer's reign ;
    And lupins are a flame, and blossom goes,
And few of the anemones remain.
And buds of foxgloves wait for June to come again.

88

Now Liberty has beaten down beneath her
    The last of the oppressors, to the dust.
And now that traitor voice that troubled ether
    Will sneer no more at what is right and just,
    And those that need a voice for crime and lust
Must hire another, if they still can pay.
    Many a voice at night on many a gust
Will howl from beast, or shrill from bird, of prey,
But not that sneering voice again after to-day.

89

Now flowers Johnny-go-to-bed-at-noon
    With its great clock beside it ; and there peer
And peep from bushes buds that know that June
    Is on her way, for in the evenings clear
    She haunts the garden as though very near.
The honeysuckle heard her step afar.
    The rose has guessed that she will soon be here,
Gliding across the lawns when daisies are
Still shut, while fades from May's last night the last pale star.

90   *May 30*

And now the scabious begins to show
    In gardens, though not yet by the roads' edges,
And candytuft is like to melting snow,
    And all the may has withered from the hedges ;
    And partly challenges and partly pledges
Cock pheasants call at evening from the grass ;
    And taller in the marshes grow the sedges ;
And, riding a South wind, light showers pass,
And the sun shines again on buttercups like brass.

91

Now figwort by a shaded avenue
    Puts forth its purple and pale-yellow bloom
Under the trees ; and monkshood grows there too,
    Giving its touch of colour to the gloom.
    Now brighter colours tint the grass's plume,
And all the fat black slugs are fully grown ;
    And late the gloaming lingers, to illume
The deep green grass, and long the moths have flown,
Like fairy ghosts, before it leaves our landscape lone.

The first flush comes to nectarines and peaches,
    Though they are hard and small and mostly green,
Dwelling in luxury beyond the reaches
    Of storm and frost ; and grapes may just be seen,
    But still so small that bunches twist and lean
This way and that, for not as yet they weigh
    Enough to hang down.   Where blue sky had been
Sweeps, like the white skirts of departing May,
A flashing shower of hail across the darkened day.

JUNE AGAIN

I

June 1

The ramblers bud, and it is June again ;
    And the wild iris stands beside the stream ;
And grass grows greener for the recent rain,
    And over it the wind with feet agleam
    Runs from the South ; and leaves of chickweed teem,
With tracks on it where waterhens have run
    Over still water ; and the tansies seem
To sparkle back a twinkle to the sun.
And honeysuckle's buds are bursting one by one.

2

On short black wings the water-ousel flies
    Down the stream's centre, as kingfishers go,
And tall beside him the red stachys rise,
    And bullrushes' great leaves like sabres show,
    And in the grass the little medicks glow.
And now ranunculus begins to creep
    Over the pathways ; and the crowsfoot grow,
Yellow and orange, in the meadows deep.
And all the blackbirds sing before they go to sleep.

3

June 2

Now Spring's wild rush of flowers is all over
    And all the blossoms have long taken flight ;
And in the meadowlands there grows the clover,
    The red kind and the yellow and the white,
    And buttercups are flashing in the light,
And dog-daisies, that all amongst the hay
    Will shine like stars upon a Summer's night,
Are coming out as stars come when the day
Is lately gone, nor yet appears the Milky Way.

180

And now the iris wither, but the bees
    Find the veronicas nigh fully blown
And lupins in their glory.   All the trees
    Glitter with light, and the rejoicing tone
    Of bird-song is about their branches thrown.
Geums are shining still, and cranesbills near.
    Gravely the dark blue monkshood stands alone.
And a delphinium begins to peer
Like a shy elf that peeps to see what else is here.

5

Now twayblade orchid rises in the shade
    And to the shadows gives a faint green glow
At a wood's edge ; and that weed strangely made,
    The marestail, by the roads begins to show,
    Last of its kind ; four million years ago
Its generation throve, and made our coal ;
    And where the great coal-forests used to grow,
Now buried by the silt that rivers roll,
This strange, small, jointed reed remains, surviving sole.

Now Canterbury bells are gleaming fair
    With every bell, in glass-protected bowers ;
While along garden paths pinks scent the air ;
    And, riding a light wind, go wandering showers,
    Setting the blackbirds singing to the flowers.
Blue poppies that the frost so nearly slew
    Turn to the light, and from the sunny hours
Gather a brightness for their lovely blue.
And sunlight flashes out like a bright dream come true.

7

At the land's edge, between the fields and sea,
    Thrift makes a long pink carpet.   In the vales
Where no man goes, and butterfly and bee
    Are undisturbed, that slope towards the rails,
    Where cuttings and embankments cross the dales,
Valerian and campion make their wild
    Untended gardens : smoke above them sails
And noise roars by, but they seem reconciled,
For never has the smoke swept clear but they have smiled.

How fortunate that Hitler never knew
    An English school ! Looking from this calm June
Back through six years, one sees it. Boys that flew
    Into a rage while fighting found out soon
    That hitting in bad temper brought no boon
To anyone, as he at Coventry
    And Bath hit blindly, like a vexed buffoon,
While our men struck at road and factory,
Till lost and broken lay the arms of Germany.

9

Now shine the scented blooms of a Scotch rose
    In an old rockery ; and, garden-bred,
A crimson potentilla darkly glows ;
    And now the lupins have begun to shed
    Their flaming blossoms. And the bees are fed
On their pale-golden flower. The small pear
    Upon a wall blushes a brighter red,
And arum lilies in the open air
Are flashing in the sun, and song is everywhere.

And the wall-speedwell's tiny bloom appears
    Where farm-walls shelter it, as though the sky
Had dropped a speck or two from its blue sphere
    To gleam with azure glory near a sty.
    The swallows do not see it, racing by :
It is too small, and they have their own blue.
    But there it glitters, and it caught my eye.
Haply small birds and beasts observe it too,
When the farmyard is hushed, but for the pigeons' coo.

And now the little-willowherb is seen
    In wilder places, and in gardens glow
The first of the sweet-peas, and through the green
    And brown and yellow of a hayfield flow
    Pale silver waves whenever the winds blow ;
And over it the swallows hunt for flies,
    Which rise in fine warm weather and sink low
For rain, before we notice cloudy skies,
And the birds follow them, visible to our eyes.

The woodcock's brood is hatched for some **few days,**
    And broken lie the bits of the brown shell,
For pale brown is the egg the woodcock lays,
    Like to the leaves that, last November, fell,
    Mottled with spots that imitate so well
The shadows among leaves ; the mother-bird
    Carries her young to feed, as those few tell
Who ever saw her, when no sound is heard
And twilight stills the woods like an unspoken word.

A single orchid has upraised its head,
    A pyramid of blossom in the hay,
Where tottie-grass has ripened, and dull red
    The clover grows, and the dog-daisies sway
    Their starry faces, and the golden day
Of buttercups is here, and the white clover
    Blooms low amid the grass, and bright and gay
The speedwell shines.   No more we hear that rover,
The cuckoo, who sang here when daffodils were over.

14

There is a hush and calm about a fall
    Of water, even in its endless roar
And even with the hurrying of all
    That it sweeps dancing downward evermore ;
    Its noise is as of something that of yore
Nursed all Earth's children, and its hurry seems
    Part of the calm of Nature and the lore
Which gives one meaning to a myriad schemes
And shows reality, firm on its base of dreams.

15

O, what a silly tale that woman writes
    Who, sitting on her cloudy promontory
Upon Parnassus, tells of dreadful nights
    When cities fell, and battles loud and gory,
    Then with an anticlimax spoils her story.
For we have heard how when the hour came
    That was to crown the allies' arms with glory,
And fortresses were going up in flame,
Herr Hitler went to church to wed some German dame.

16

So history goes, and it is hard sometimes
    To find significance in what men do.
What had historians said if through gay chimes
    Napoleon charged to church from Waterloo ?
    Or if some bride of Tamerlane's once threw
Her wedding bouquet on his heap of skulls ?
    Surely this new tale is absurd though true,
Some little flippancy Bellona culls
As her car roars away from where the battle lulls.

17

June 10

Veronicas are all in bloom to-day,
    With buds above the blossoms and, below,
Circles of petals lying on the clay,
    And quantities of bees about them go.
    And still the lupins flare like a long row
Of many-coloured flames ; and one by one
    The azure blossoms of the larkspur show,
While the sweetwilliams open to the sun.
And on syringa's boughs the budding has begun.

18

June 11

The cuckoo-spit is hanging white on weeds ;
    Portuguese laurel is a misty haze
Of buds unopened ; and the plantain's seeds
    Blossom about its dark head ; and the days
    Of Spring are over. Now the mallows raise
Their shining faces ; and a swarm of bees
    Hangs on a pergola amongst a maze
Of roses, all in bud. And now one sees
The Summer's soberer green upon the darkening trees.

19

And in the dreamy hush of Summertime
    Goes Earth upon her journey through the stars
And nears the spot where I began this rhyme,
    Spinning in space with all her ghastly scars,
    A battered orb that Venus sees and Mars
Perhaps with wonder. Slowly the scars mend,
    Slowly Earth ceases for a while her wars
And turns again, her crops and herds to tend.
War and peace, night and day, are with her to the end.

20

Now the herb-bennet forms dark purple burrs
    Covered with little hooks ; and pink and white
The snowberry's little bloom shows ; and the furze
    Is seeding ; and the bloom is all alight
    On that strange flower, rarely in our sight,
Called the French thistle, its pale golden domes,
    All veined with purple, rising to a height
Of some feet, where the rabbits have their homes
In a grey sandpit's wall, and nothing else there roams.

21

Hundreds of blooms of the strange flower grow
    On that sand wall, and elsewhere none are known
By any of us here. Two years ago
    Under a dun of grey sand it had grown,
    And next year with its whole wild tribe had flown
To where it is, four hundred yards from there,
    A thing to seek out for the sight alone,
Not for the scent, for, though the flower is fair,
Its acrid odour fills with bitterness the air.

                June 12

The ermine moths are out ; a ghost-moth's wing
    Lies on a path ; a cactus, like a rose
With pale blue petals spread, is flowering.
    One red-and-yellow bell in fullness blows,
    The rest are buds in a green spray that goes
Down from a single stalk, while under glass
    The cactus dreams of where the forest grows
That is all cactus, and the plains of grass
Flash in the sun beyond, and Kenya's rivers pass.

A yellow vetch is shining in the hay,
    And all the buttercups are past their prime,
And crowsfoot thrives, and all along the way
    Cow-parsnip prospers ; and it is the time
    When honeysuckle blooms, whose tendrils climb
Among the roses, which are not yet grown,
    And elders blossom, and the things my rhyme
Began with have again about us grown,
And silver waves and brown across the hay are blown.

A yellow scabious six feet in height
    Is blossoming, and still the lupins flare
Like flames whose colours may surprise the night,
    Rising from embers with a coloured glare
    Because some curious chemical is there
Within the timbers, or a passer-by.
    Has cast it on them, wandering from where
None knows and passing on to mystery
And darkness. Just so flare the lupins ere they die.

25

To-day two men who fought for Liberty,
    Deserting those who would not lift a hand
To help her, must for that desertion be
    Sentenced before Court Martial in the land
Where such things happen, where men understand
How just the sentence, as in all the world
    No others can. Indeed a mad world, and
But barely saved. Next time we may be hurled
Over the edge, these two keeping their war-flag furled.

26

Blackberry blossoms glimmer by the way,
    And the wild roses from the hedges peer ;
And spotted orchids light the growing hay,
    And, darker pink, the pyramids appear ;
    And thistles with their crimson heads are here ;
And crowsfoot, hawkweed and dog-daisies grow
    Among the meadows ; and the circling year
Brings on the foxglove, whose red splendours show
Along dim glades of woods and make their shadows glow.

27

And Canterbury bells are at their best,
    And privet by the roads is all in bud,
And now syringa wakes from its long rest,
    Blossom by blossom ; and a small blue flood
    Of petals still is lying on the mud
Under veronicas ; and columbines
    Show all their splendour, and the tall monkshood.
And grapes are hanging straighter on the vines.
And through tall flowers here and there the bindweed twines.

And now Earth comes again to where she span
 When I, while other workers cut the hay,
To tell her flowery journey first began.
 It cannot be she tarries on the way,
 And yet it is as though she did delay
When April's bitter nights about her froze.
 Like mortal travellers in snow astray,
Battered and weary, as though late, she goes.
Yet war and frost and storm, how well, how well she knows.

29

And as she comes again into mid-June,
 And nearly into peace, I drop my pen,
At evening as there shines a crescent moon,
 Leaving a mighty tale for other men,
 Who for a hundred years may write, and then
Not tell the story of this wondrous year,
 When Liberty from exile turned, and when
The tyrant toppled from his throne of fear,
Whose shadow was so long and reached how very near.

THE   END

www.ingramcontent.com/pod-product-compliance
Lightning Source LLC
Chambersburg PA
CBHW030932090426
42737CB00007B/395